For the Life of the World

FOR THE **LIFE** OF THE **WORLD**

INVITED TO EUCHARISTIC MISSION

BISHOP ANDREW COZZENS AND TIM GLEMKOWSKI

Our Sunday Visitor
Huntington, Indiana

Our Sunday Visitor Publishing Division
Our Sunday Visitor, Inc.
200 Noll Plaza
Huntington, IN 46750
www.osv.com
1-800-348-2440

ISBN: 978-1-63966-231-9 (Inventory No. T2914)
1. RELIGION / Christianity / Catholic
2. RELIGION / Christian Ministry / Evangelism
3. RELIGION / Christian Rituals & Practice / Sacraments
eISBN: 978-1-63966-232-6
LCCN: 2024935242

Cover design: 5 Stones
Interior design: Amanda Falk

PRINTED IN THE UNITED STATES OF AMERICA

Contents

Preface

The most important things that have happened in my life seem to have fallen into my lap. Although I had the privilege of leading the National Eucharistic Revival on behalf of the U.S. bishops, it wasn't actually my idea. I have come to believe that even before the bishops thought of the idea, the Holy Spirit was moving the Church to respond to the challenges of our times.

Many will remember hearing about the Pew Research findings released in the fall of 2019 about Catholics and the Eucharist. These findings indicated that nearly 70 percent of Catholics did not believe in the Real Presence of Christ in the Eucharist. This data disturbed the whole Church, and many bishops were especially concerned. As Church leaders reflected on the results of this survey, further questions were raised, not only about what Catholics believe, but also about how the research was conducted. To dig deeper, the leaders of the Eucharistic Revival worked with the McGrath Institute of the University of Notre Dame to sponsor another study in 2022 through the Center for Applied Research in the Apostolate. CARA's data painted a somewhat better picture, but the overall news still indicated a serious disconnect. While perhaps as many as 60 percent of self-identified Catholics said they understood the Church's teaching on the Real Presence, only 17 percent of them attended Mass every Sunday. Clearly, even if someone expresses belief in the Eucharist, if they don't attend Mass on Sunday, then they have not yet encountered Jesus Christ alive in the Eucharist.

The initial Pew study was deeply disturbing to many bishops, and it was widely discussed at the bishops' meeting in November 2019. Coming from this deep concern was a sense that action was needed. In the hearts of many bishops, a fire was beginning to burn. Bishop Robert Barron, at the time the chair of the Committee on Evangelization and Catechesis, put together a proposal for a three-year Eucharistic renewal. Because I had just been elected to lead that committee in the next term, I took part in some initial meetings with the leaders of the bishops' conference during January and February 2020. There was a lot of support for developing an initiative that might impact the Church at every level. The plan was to bring a proposal to the bishops in June 2020.

However, in March 2020, the world changed. The eruption of the COVID-19 pandemic shut everything down, and our efforts were put on hold. During that time we lived through the incredible tragedy of the inability to have public Mass. This forced disconnect from the

Eucharist only increased the crisis in the Church. When the bishops were finally able to gather in November 2020, and we were finally able to present a plan, it was clear we needed a revival, and most bishops considered it providential that we had already begun to envision it. I became chair of the Committee on Evangelization and Catechesis and was given the job of building it.

That spring, we began consulting dozens of Catholic leaders all over the country about what we might do. Tim Glemkowski helped me facilitate dozens of meetings. I admit I was surprised by the strength of the response. Evangelistic, diocesan, and parish leaders believed now was the time for a national movement. The response was so encouraging that we began to wonder whether God was going to do something big through this revival, something bigger than we knew.

We brought the proposal to all the bishops over the course of our gatherings in 2021. We proposed a three-year plan for revival that would affect the Church at every level: the parish, the diocese, and the nation. At its center was the plan for a National Eucharistic Congress for up to eighty thousand people. I had my doubts about how the bishops would vote because it was such a large undertaking. But when the final vote was 201 to 12, I knew the Holy Spirit wanted this revival.

As the Revival began to spread, and I and other evangelistic leaders traveled the country, we saw a response which we could not have anticipated. We saw engagement at the diocesan and parish levels beyond what we could have imagined. We saw apostolates from across the country wanting to be involved. We were able to plan and execute the first ever National Eucharistic Pilgrimage, which processed the Blessed Sacrament from the North, South, East, and West and allowed hundreds of thousands of people to encounter Jesus Christ in the Eucharist on the way to 10th National Eucharistic Congress. We have become convinced that the Revival is not meant to be just another program, but a movement. We became convinced that the Eucharist is central to evangelization. We have come to believe that God wants to renew his Church through individual Catholics being renewed in their hearts by coming to live fully Eucharistic lives. The Eucharist is the heart of the Church, and when people encounter the love of Jesus Christ truly present in the Eucharist, they are changed. They never leave the Church because they know there is nowhere else where they can encounter him in this way. When they truly understand a Eucharistic life, they become missionaries — Eucharistic missionaries.

We want to encourage and fan into flame this work we feel the Holy Spirit doing. We don't really know where it will lead, except to a more vibrant, evangelistic Church. We hope you will discover in this book how to live a fully Eucharistic life and experience the call we have experienced, to become a Eucharistic missionary.

Most Rev. Andrew Cozzens
Bishop of Crookston
February 20, 2024

CHAPTER 1

Starting a Fire

In the Gospel of Luke, Jesus exclaims, "I have come to set the earth on fire, and how I wish it were already blazing!" (Lk 12:49). What is this fire about which Our Lord speaks? It is the fire that burned in the heart of God before time began, the fire that is the love between the Father and the Son: the Holy Spirit. It is the fire of love that moved God to create us in an act of sheer goodness so that we could share in his own divine life.[1]

And when we wandered far from God, this fire drove God to come after us, to take on flesh and dwell among us. This fire then burned in the human heart of Jesus, and it burned with a desire to heal the pain of sin, to destroy death, and to bring us back to God.

At the Last Supper, Jesus said to his apostles, "I have eagerly desired to eat this Passover with you before I suffer" (Lk 22:15). Why did he desire to eat this Passover? Because this was the moment when he would share his divine life with us — the life that could heal us and unite us again with him — the life that overcomes death. This Passover was the fulfillment of his mission.

This divine fire is expressed in the words which are the center of the Last Supper and the center of the Mass: "This is my body which will be given up for you. ... This is the chalice of my blood, the blood of the new and eternal covenant, which will be poured out for you and for many ..." Jesus longed to give himself for us and to us, so that we could share his life forever. But to do this, he had to pass through death. He had to allow this fire to consume him totally. We must never forget that it cost Jesus his life to give us the Eucharist.

Imagine his dead body lying in the tomb in the middle of the night as Easter Sunday dawns. Jesus has poured out his life completely, and it seems there is now nothing left. Then this fire, this love, by which he had taken on flesh in Mary's womb, now brings his dead body back to life and fills it with glory. He has conquered death, the gates of hell lie broken, and he comes out of the tomb with one desire: to spread this fire burning in him throughout the whole world.

The apostles and the earliest disciples were bewildered and discouraged by the death of Jesus. They did not understand why he had to pass through death to bring about new life. As he told two of his disciples the day of his resurrection on the way to Emmaus, "Was it not necessary that the Messiah should suffer these things and enter into his glory?" (Lk 24:26). Though they did not recognize him, he showed them the meaning of the Last Supper, his death, and his resurrection. As they approached the place where they were going, they begged him, "Stay with us." And he did stay with them. He came into the house and "took bread, said the blessing, broke it, and gave it to them. With that their eyes were opened, and they recognized him" (vv. 30–31). They encountered him in the Eucharist, and this encounter changed them. Now that they recognized him in the breaking of the bread, their hearts were on fire, too. And they ran back to Jerusalem to share the good news of this encounter.

This fire of God's love is a "consuming fire" (Heb 12:29). This fire has the power to change you if you encounter it, if you surrender to it. This fire is what has the power to change the world. In the Eucharist, Jesus wants to set our hearts on fire with his love and turn us into his missionaries. Just like those first disciples at Emmaus, we can be transformed by this encounter and sent to share this good news.

What is a Eucharistic missionary?

A Eucharistic missionary is someone who has encountered the living Jesus Christ in the Eucharist and been transformed by him. He has decided to make Jesus Christ the Lord of his life. A Eucharistic missionary lives the essence of the Eucharistic mystery through encountering Jesus' presence, living Jesus' communion, and making a gift of his life through Jesus' sacrifice.

We have come to describe this life of a Eucharistic missionary in four pillars: 1) Eucharistic Encounter, leading to 2) Eucharistic Identity, poured out in 3) a Eucharistic Life, all on the way to 4) Eucharistic Mission. These pillars describe a path of transformation patterned on the Eucharistic mystery that brings a person into the depth of being a missionary. They conform us more to Jesus and allow us to grow into fully sharing his life. In this way these pillars are foundational for every spiritual journey and deeply rooted in our Catholic tradition.

Pope Francis spoke about this transformation in a Wednesday General Audience in 2017. He pointed out, as many saints have before him, that the actions Scripture always uses to describe the Eucharist — *taken*, *blessed*, *broken*, and *given* — are a description of what happened to Jesus himself, and a description of the transformation that the Lord wants to do in us:

> Does not Jesus' entire history perhaps lie in this series of gestures? And is there not in every Eucharist, also the symbol of what the Church should be? Jesus takes us, blesses us, 'breaks' our life — because there is no love without sacrifice — and offers it to others; he offers it to everyone.[2]

A Eucharistic missionary has been taken by a **Eucharistic Encounter**. He or she realizes in a real and unshakable way, that Jesus in the Eucharist is not an analogy or idea, nor a dispassionate and detached divinity, but a real, living person. And this person is deeply interested in each of us. He wants to know us, to be united with us, and wants to take us on an adventure.

In this profound encounter we are blessed, we come to know, not only who Jesus in the Eucharist is, but who we are. We come to recognize our deepest and truest **Eucharistic Identity**. This is true for each of us: Who I am is profoundly impacted by the fact that he has poured out his life for me in the Eucharist. The truth of the encounter with Jesus Christ reveals who we are in light of the unshakable reality of his love. When our identity is refounded in Christ, rooted in the truth of his love, we are able to become who he is calling us to be for the world today. This identity in Christ is the secret strength of the saints.

This Eucharistic Identity is then lived out in what can be called a **Eucharistic Life** — the unique life of a Eucharistic missionary. It is a life of communion with Jesus and with one another, which flows from the Eucharist. Most importantly, it is a life of self-gift, in imitation of Jesus' sacrifice, which is made present again at every holy Mass. We allow ourselves to be broken with him through our own self-gift, and we are invited to unite the whole content of our lives with his sacrifice for the salvation of the world. This participation in Jesus' sacrifice is what makes any mission fruitful.

Finally, we are given in **Eucharistic Mission**. We are sent from the Eucharistic banquet to bring the love found there to everyone we encounter. Because everyone, whether they know it or not, longs for what is found in the Eucharist. As baptized Catholics, each of us has a critically important part to play in this symphonic work of God. The adventure of mission on which God is calling each of us far surpasses our natural capacities and requires that we surrender to the work of God in our life.

Over the next several chapters, we will invite you to go with us on a journey to becoming a Eucharistic missionary. You may have made part of this journey already, but we need to know this path well if we are going to help others walk it, and we are always called deeper into the life of self-gift which the Eucharist teaches. We invite you to follow this path, which over time we believe will allow you to be healed, converted, formed, and unified by an encounter with Jesus in the Eucharist — and sent out on mission for the life of the world.

Questions to pray with and ponder

- Have you encountered Jesus Christ truly alive and present in the Eucharist? How has this encounter changed you?
- Consider the disciples at Emmaus, and how their hearts were set on fire by their encounter with Jesus. Do you believe Jesus wants to set your heart on fire? What would it take for you to let him?

CHAPTER 2

Why the Church Needs Eucharistic Missionaries

The Mother Cabrini Shrine, tucked away in the foothills outside Golden, Colorado, is a hidden gem, one of the important sites of American Catholicism. The property itself is unremarkable, with a simple chapel, a couple of buildings for retreats, and pleasant grounds for walking around on a sunny, breezy Colorado day. Mother Cabrini negotiated the sale of the property in 1910, in order to turn it into a summer camp for her female students. Always resourceful, she got a great deal on the land because it lacked a critical resource in the dry Western climate: water.

Sometime after she purchased the property, some of the sisters who worked with Mother Cabrini were complaining about the unreliable water supply on the property and the difficulties it caused. Mother simply

17

pointed to a spot on the ground and told them, "Lift that rock and dig." To this day, a spring runs from that exact spot — a miracle on that arid land.

Mother Frances Xavier Cabrini was a remarkable figure. Born near Milan, Italy, and driven by the desire to become a missionary, she dreamed of going to China to preach the Gospel. Pope Leo XIII talked her into going to the United States instead. Until her death in 1917, she would travel across the United States (and the world), relentlessly advocating for underprivileged youths and immigrants, founding sixty-seven different orphanages, schools, and hospitals.

What motivates great missionary saints like Mother Cabrini? Where do they come from? Are they born this way, completely different from the rest of us and inaccessible in their virtue and excellence? How do they accomplish such incredible things for the Kingdom? The reality is, what the saints experience and do is supposed to be the normal expression of life for every baptized Catholic. We who have been baptized into the death and resurrection of Jesus Christ are each called to similar dizzying heights of holiness. The saints show us our own vocation, inviting and inspiring us to fulfill this mandate that has been placed over our lives.

Through baptism, God has chosen us and set us apart to become something remarkable. As Jesus tells his followers, "It was not you who chose me, but I who chose you and appointed you to go and bear fruit that will remain" (Jn 15:16). He has spoken his purpose over our lives. Yet the lofty heights of this calling can be disorienting and frightening. Most days we are just trying to survive, to get by, and we don't have the time or the energy to think about fulfilling our divine mission.

So how do the saints like Mother Cabrini do what they do? Mother Cabrini herself summarized what compelled her: "I *will go anywhere* and *do anything* in order to *communicate* the love of Jesus to those who *do* not know him or have forgotten him." This is why the saints are who they are. They have encountered something so beautiful, compelling, and transforming — namely, the love of Jesus, fully present in the Eucharist — that they are impelled onward to extend that love to other people. This evangelization is not "proselytism." It is, as evangelical pastor D. T. Niles put it, nothing more than "one beggar telling another beggar where to find bread."

One of the most convincing witnesses to the transforming power of the Most Blessed Sacrament is Blessed Carlo Acutis (1991–2006). Carlo's parents were not particularly religious people and did not actively practice the Faith. After receiving his first holy Communion, however, Carlo fell in love with Jesus in the Eucharist. He asked his parents to take him on pilgrimages to shrines of the saints and places known for Eucharistic miracles. He even managed to convince his parents and other family members to accompany him to daily Mass.

Like many of his peers, Carlo enjoyed video games and computer programming. His early attempts to share his deep devotion to the Eucharist with friends were not successful. But when he told them about Eucharistic miracles, they became intrigued. So, he built a website to catalog and promote Eucharistic miracles online. His faith eventually brought his parents back to the Church. Then, when he was fifteen years old, Carlo was diagnosed with leukemia. He offered his suffering to God for the pope and the Church. He died in 2006.

Carlo was a Eucharistic missionary. Jesus changed Carlo's life, and his devotion to the Eucharist gave him a purpose and a mission. His parents were brought back to the Faith through him. Friends and neighbors in Milan were inspired by his example. People around the world have been influenced by his website, and the impact of this exceptional young man continues to grow. When Jesus changes a person's life, everything and everyone is better for it. The life of Carlo Acutis shows us that God is still in the business of transformation. Jesus draws close to us and calls us to draw close to him so that he can make us all that he intended us to be.

A missionary renewal of hearts

Jesus in the Eucharist has a mission. He is about something, in this scandalous act of giving us his very self. He is after our hearts. He wants us to know him personally and to encounter the love he has for us, which is capable of creating galaxies. He is after our hearts, first and foremost, for our own sake. He is the answer to every question and longing of the human heart, and he loves us desperately.

Jesus is also after our hearts for *their* sake — for the sake of the world. If our encounter with Jesus in the Eucharist is authentic, the intimacy we find there will transform us, little by little, and our hearts will be broken open. This is the process we describe in this book, from encounter, to identity, to a sacrificial life, to a missionary. If we follow this process, we will find ourselves, like Mother Cabrini and Carlo Acutis, coming to care deeply about those who do not know, or have forgotten, Jesus' love. We will find ourselves being led, subtly at first, but steadily more and more, on mission.

Today, especially, the Church is being called to a missionary renewal as the culture moves further and further away from Christianity. This means that all we do and how we think, from our structures to ways of living, must be suitably set up for a time of mission. The world does not need another strategic plan. It needs saints, missionary disciples, Catholics who have plumbed the depths of what Christ came to bring, "life and [to] have it more abundantly" (Jn 10:10), so that they can be witnesses to the world of the difference Christ makes.

God has a plan for the renewal of his Church, today, and the healing of the world that is so desperately needed. His plan involves each of us. In different ways each of us is called to be his missionary. We believe this call flows from a deep encounter with the Jesus Christ living in the Eucharist, and that many are being called in a deeper way to be Eucharistic missionaries, choosing to live a life of missional fruitfulness flowing from his total self-gift in the Eucharist. It is a form of authentic Catholic holiness and missionary fruitfulness, perhaps uniquely suitable today.

Living in apostolic times

It is clear to anyone who is watching with Christian eyes that our world is in crisis. From international wars and the scourge of injustice to confusion about the human person and the disintegration of the family, thick darkness covers the earth. In our own country, an intense struggle is underway for the hearts and souls of our young people. Strong cultural forces are pulling many away from God. And these crises are affecting our Church, which is also wounded and hurting.

How should we respond? The problems of our time are spiritual, and they demand a spiritual response. Only the healing power of Christ's love can help us. As Catholics, we know where to find that power and his presence: in the holy Eucharist.

Our times are not the only difficult times. In 1902, just one year before his death, Pope Leo XIII wrote an encyclical on the Eucharist: *Mirae Caritatis*. Pope Leo had received a kind of prophetic vision that the twentieth century would be one of great evil, in which the enemy would be powerful. Because of this vision, he ordered that the Prayer to St. Michael the Archangel be prayed after every Low Mass in the whole Church. Noting that there were many things he could focus on at the end of his long pontificate — many problems he could address — Pope Leo chose to focus on strengthening the Church at her very center. He invited the whole Church to focus on the Eucharist, which is the true heart of the Church.

Pope Leo's words are just as important for us today. We are encountering so many deep problems in the world. We are experiencing so much division and struggle within the Church. As the heart of the Church, the Eucharist pumps the life of God to the members of the Church. Just like a body needs a healthy heart, and all the members of the body need to be connected to the heart to function properly, if the Body of Christ is to be strong, to stand against the darkness in our world, the members need to be strong in their Eucharistic faith. If the Church is strong in her Eucharistic faith, the fire of love that burns in the heart of Christ will burn in the hearts of her members.

The Catholic Church today faces many temptations: to beat a steady retreat toward irrelevance; to hunker down and ride out the secularizing storm; or to fight fire with fire, demonizing our opponents, becoming trapped in partisan power plays. Instead, we must respond to the divine invitation that is offered to us: Against all apparent odds, the Church is being invited on mission.

The Gospel has not lost its effectiveness, even if more creative modes of expressing it are required to get beyond the defense mechanisms of a weary world. Jesus Christ is no less risen from the dead today than he was when the early Church baptized the entire ancient world in a matter of centuries. God sees the problems in the world today, and he is not worried. He is not anxious. He is on the move.

"I have come to set the earth on fire, and how I wish it were already blazing!" (Lk 12:49). The fire of love that burns in Jesus' heart is present in the Eucharist, and he wants to share that same fire with us. Our encounter with Christ in the Eucharist is meant to move us *outward*.

We believe that God is calling Eucharistic missionaries who will burn with this same desire of Jesus. Do you want this fire to burn in you? Draw near to him in the Eucharist and he will set your heart on fire for his mission. Our hope for you reading this book is that you will be drawn into a deeper encounter with Christ in the Eucharist and experience a deep renewal in the understanding of your own identity in Christ. Renewed in this identity, you will desire to make a gift of your life, through, with, and in Christ. All this will make you a missionary filled with the strength of his Eucharistic love. You will find yourself saying with Mother Cabrini, "I will go anywhere and do anything in order to communicate the love of Jesus to those who do not know him or have forgotten him."

If the mission of the Church is to be fruitful, it will be because of people who love the Eucharist and want to live a life formed by the Eucharist. The mission of Christ depends on inviting every Catholic to a deeper encounter with the Eucharist. The fire we have ignited and experienced together cannot spread without each one of us. And we must continue to spread the great gift God has given us until all have been offered a deeper encounter with Christ in the Eucharist.

Questions to pray with and ponder

- How does it make you feel to learn that God is calling you to missionary fruitfulness, just as he called Mother Cabrini and Carlo Acutis? What might that fruitfulness look like in your life?
- Are there people in your life who have been transformed by their encounter with Jesus in the Eucharist? How has the encounter changed them and sent them outward to draw others to Christ?

CHAPTER 3

Who Is Jesus, and What Did He Come to Do?

God desires to encounter you. While it is possible to encounter God wherever we are, he has blessed us with special means that become vehicles of his presence. These include creation, the Scriptures, the poor, the community of faith, the sacraments — but especially the Eucharist. In the Eucharist, Jesus keeps the promise he made on the Mount of Olives before his ascension: "Behold, I am with you always, until the end of the age" (Mt 28:20).

We meet Jesus, truly present in the Eucharist, when we receive him at Mass or spend time with him in adoration. What we encounter is not just an idea, but a person. This encounter is meant to transform us. It is the essential first step to discipleship. And we have to understand why. If we want to understand what it means to be a Eucharistic missionary, in imitation of Jesus, we have to go back to two very basic questions: Who is Jesus? And what did he come to do?

Really, everything we do as Catholics — everything the Church teaches, believes, celebrates, and practices — comes down to understanding these two vitally important questions. But in order to answer these questions about Jesus fully, we have to step back even further. We have to understand God the Father.

Jesus often explained his own life on earth and his ministry in reference to the Father:

- "I came from God and am here; I did not come on my own, but he sent me." (John 8:42)
- "The words that I speak to you I do not speak on my own. The Father who dwells in me is doing his works." (John 14:10)
- "As the Father has sent me, so I send you." (John 20:21)

Jesus clearly understood his public ministry as carrying out the will of the Father. He was not at work on his own, but his ministry was a partnership. The Father sent him to do something, and he was about that work every day. What did the Father send him to do? The Father sent Jesus, who sent the Church, who gives us the Eucharist, for a singular purpose: to bring his children home.

"Where are you?"

Perhaps the most heartbreaking words in Scripture are those spoken by God to Adam, after Adam and Eve ate of the forbidden fruit, when "the eyes of both of them were opened, and they knew that they were naked" (Gn 3:7). God then asks Adam, "Where are you?" (v. 9).

To understand the full impact of these words, we have to go back all the way to the beginning, when creation began. Science tells us that, 13.8 billion years ago, light began rushing forth from a single point in the universe in an explosion so powerful that the universe is still expanding outward from this initial action today. We call this phenomenon the "big bang," first posited by Abbé Georges Lemaître, a Catholic priest and personal friend of Albert Einstein. The Book of Genesis puts it this way: "In the beginning, when God created the heavens and the earth — and the earth was without form or shape, with darkness over the abyss and a mighty wind sweeping over the waters — Then God said: Let there be light" (1:1–3).

Why did God choose to create beginning with light 13.8 billion years ago? Well, in order to understand the reason for any sequence of actions, you have to go to the very last thing that happens, which makes sense of all of the previous actions. This is a basic philosophical principle, often stated thus: "The first in intention is the last in execution." For example, if you want to go on a bike ride, actually riding your bike is the very last thing that happens in a sequence of actions, which includes telling your family you are going on a bike ride, taking the bike out of the garage, putting on a helmet, etc. The first thing you intended to do — ride a bike — is actually the last thing you end up doing.

This is what we see in the creation account, unfolding in the first two chapters of Genesis. It's a symphonic outpouring of the creative power of God: stars, quintillions of them, and galaxies, then the Earth, first formed, then populated, coming into being. Each time God makes something, he keeps going; he's not done yet. Then, on the sixth day, he forms man and woman, and when he is finished, he … rests. He rests because he's done. At last, 13.8 billion years of the creative action of an all-powerful being are consummated, accomplished. The first in intention — human beings — is now the last in execution. All of it — every star, galaxy, animal, and plant — was actually pressing toward the creation of humanity. Why?

To state it plainly: love. God, who is Love, conceived of every possible multiverse that could ever exist, and he saw the one that had you in it, and he said, "Let there be light." Billions of years ago, before there were stars, God made those so he could make you. What does this mean? It means every hair on your head is counted. It means that you can relax, that you can breathe.

These first parents of ours were not just made, but they were made to have *life*. In the beginning of the story of the human race, Adam and Eve experienced the fullness of life they were made for. God "blew into his nostrils the breath of life, and the man became a living being" (Gn 2:7). This breath of God in man exploded into a life of adventure. Human beings were made for freedom, for joy, for laughter. They began to shape and explore the Garden they had been given, to make it an even more interesting place. "At the breezy time of day" (3:8), Genesis tells us, God himself would come and walk in the Garden with Adam and Eve. They experienced mutual delight in each other's presence. The Father delighted in them, and they in the love of their Father. They were safe and whole and good.

But then something terrible happened. The devil, a fallen angel, in his own pride unable to serve, hates the Father more than anything. And the easiest way to strike at any father's heart? Go after his kids. In his cunning, as we read at the beginning of Genesis 3, the devil came into the Garden and attacked human beings — not in an outright attack, but by striking at their trust in God.

In order for there to be love in the Garden, there had to be freedom and choice. To be forced into a relationship is not real love at all. That's why God gave the man and woman one rule, or, perhaps better put, a door handle. If Adam and Eve ever wanted to step *out* of the love relationship with God, they were free to do so. Thus, when God gave this prohibition, he emphasized their freedom: "You are free to eat from any of the trees of the garden except the tree of knowledge of good and evil. From that tree you shall not eat; when you eat from it you shall die" (Gn 2:16–17).

God wasn't being punitive or petty, and he certainly was not saying he would kill them. He was simply articulating a state of affairs. We might compare it to parents today telling kids not to play in the street. This rule does not stem from a repressive ideology, but from care. Parents don't want their kids to get hit by a car. In the Garden, God knew what would enter into their lives if they chose to grab the door handle and step out of the relationship with him. This objective reality was death — a power that would come to rule over them, should they choose to leave.

God gave his children freedom to eat from any tree in the Garden, except for one. The devil tempted Eve by overemphasizing the rigidity of the rule. "Did God really say, 'You shall not eat from any of the trees in the garden?'" (3:1). He took aim at their trust in God, and we see the broken trust in Eve's response. She added to the rule God gave them: "We may eat of the fruit of the trees in the garden; it is only about the fruit of the tree in the middle of the garden that God said, 'You shall not eat it *or even touch it*, or else you will die'" (3:2–3, emphasis added). God never said anything about "touching." But we tend to overemphasize the unfairness of our parents when we feel we are being kept from something we want. Eve then took of the fruit and ate it. Next, she turned to offer it to Adam, and he ate, too.

Immediately, something changed in them, and we know this because they "hid themselves" (3:8). In that moment, Adam and Eve chose to step out of the Father's house. From their free choice, every pestilence, every war, every violent action, every manipulation and crime, every trauma that will ever happen, was unleashed upon humanity. Thousands of years of human history would unfold waiting for God to come and save us. God's question in Genesis 3:9, "Where are you?", is the aching cry of a Father who has had his children taken away from him.

Jesus himself is a missionary

Seeing the world broken in so many ways by sin, the answer of the Trinity was to send God the Son into the world to reclaim the world for himself. Jesus came to break the reign of sin and establish the new and eternal covenant — a covenant that was prepared for in the Old Testament and is fulfilled in the Eucharist. Jesus came to free us from slavery to sin and fill us with his life. Those who believe in Jesus and are incorporated into his body are able to share in this new and eternal life.

Of course, we know that many people in the Church today are "sacramentalized but not evangelized" — that is, they may have been baptized and received first Communion, and they may even go to Mass, but they do not experience the new life that Jesus came to share. Jesus is not the center of their life, and they do not live intentinally as his disciples. They still live trapped in their sins and in some way are hiding from God, whether consciously or unconsciously. This is because they have not encountered Jesus Christ as a real and living person who knows them and offers them a new life.

Jesus is not just an idea, and "being Christian is not the result of an ethical choice or a lofty idea, but the encounter with an event, a person, which gives life a new horizon and a decisive direction."[1] This is one of the main reasons Jesus remains with us in the Eucharist, so we can encounter him alive and experience the transformative power of his love.

Questions to pray with and ponder

- Who is Jesus?
- What did he come to do?

CHAPTER 4

Encounter Changes Everything

Pope Francis speaks about the encounter with Jesus in the strongest terms: "Christian faith is either an encounter with him alive, or it does not exist."[1] Why does he say this? To experience true conversion, we need to encounter Jesus Christ, the God Man who is alive. All that we have talked about in terms of Christ's mission will remain theoretical, an interesting idea, until we realize Jesus Christ is alive today and that he knows us and calls us to follow him. Salvation is not only a "what," but a "who."

It is one of the stunning realities when you think about the life of Jesus. Tens of thousands of people heard Jesus preach, saw his miraculous healings, maybe even ate some food he miraculously multiplied, and they went home and said to themselves: "Wow, that was interesting. That Jesus guy, he is really something." But it did not affect their hearts or change their lives.

But then there are other encounters in Scripture. Encounters like Jesus has with Peter or Matthew when he calls them, and they leave everything and follow him. Or encounters like he had with Mary Magdalene or the woman caught in adultery. In these instances people were changed, transformed.

Zacchaeus, after encountering Jesus said, "Behold, half of my possessions, Lord, I shall give to the poor, and if I have extorted anything from anyone I shall repay it four times over" (Lk 19:8). The woman at the well went running back to town, saying: "Come see a man who told me everything I have done. Could he possibly be the Messiah?" (Jn 4:29). The encounter with Jesus changed them.

"We have found the Messiah"

Let's look at one of these encounters in-depth. In the first chapter of John's Gospel, we read the story of the first encounter the apostles Andrew and John had with Jesus. Andrew and John already had a religious instinct. They were disciples of John the Baptist and were spending time with him in the Judean desert, learning his message of repentance. One day when they were with John, everything changed. John the Baptist saw Jesus walking by and said, "Behold the Lamb of God" (1:36). John's Jewish disciples knew the importance of the Passover Lamb — the Lamb of God. Intrigued, John and Andrew walked after Jesus. This led to an encounter.

As they were walking behind him, "Jesus turned and saw them following him and said to them, 'What are you looking for?' They said to him, 'Rabbi' (which translated means Teacher), 'where are you staying?' He said to them, 'Come, and you will see.' So they went and saw where he was staying, and they stayed with him that day. It was about four in the afternoon" (vv. 38–39). Recounting this story in his Gospel, John includes even the detail of the time of day. Could it be that this was such a life-changing moment for him that he always remembered the exact moment it happened? From 4:00 p.m. on that day, his life would never be the same.

What was so life-changing about that encounter? They spent the day with Jesus, and the Gospel doesn't tell us exactly what happened. But we know that, as they talked with Jesus that day, these two men began to realize that he was different than anyone they had ever met. He was the answer to questions they didn't know they had. They began to see that Jesus spoke to the deepest desires and needs of their hearts. Eventually, they realized that they could not live without him. Within a matter of hours with Jesus, they were willing to stake their whole life on him.

Andrew was so affected by this day with Jesus that he went and found his brother Peter and told him, "We have found the Messiah" (v. 41). Andrew, like every religious Jew, was waiting and hoping for the Messiah, the savior who would restore freedom and salvation to God's people. Andrew was convinced that Jesus was this man. He and John both came to recognize that in Jesus they had met someone divine. It would take them time to fully articulate it, but in Jesus they were encountering God, and everything changed. Their whole lives had to be reoriented now. They had encountered "an event, a person, which gives life a new horizon and a decisive direction."[2] This encounter with Jesus is the heart of Christianity.

Elements of the encounter with Jesus

The encounter with Jesus takes on different forms for different people. Some people are healed, like blind Bartimaeus and the lepers; others have their sins forgiven, like Mary Magdalene. But the result is the same: Through this encounter, they realize who Jesus is and that they cannot live without him, and they seek to become his disciple.

There are four essential elements to this encounter:

1. The realization that Jesus is God
2. The experience of my own unworthiness
3. The discovery that I am intimately loved
4. The invitation to follow him in a new life

First is the realization that Jesus is God. Take, for example, Peter's encounter with Jesus in Luke 5. Peter is just getting to know Jesus, really. Jesus is preaching on the shore of the sea as Simon Peter cleans his nets. As the crowd grows bigger, Jesus asks Peter if he can get into his boat to continue to teach. We don't know what Jesus was saying as he preached, but Simon Peter must have been listening. Then, Jesus looks at Peter and says, "Put out into deep water and lower your nets for a catch" (Lk 5:4). Peter hesitates, explaining that they fished all night and caught nothing, but, ultimately, he agrees and puts out into the deep and lowers the nets. The catch of fish is so great that they have to call their partners in another boat to come and help them, and they fear their nets will break. Simon Peter is astounded. He realizes he is before no ordinary man. He turns to Jesus and calls him "Lord" (*Adonai* in Hebrew, which is used for the Divine). He says, "Depart from me, Lord, for I am a sinful man" (v. 8).

This brings us to the second essential element of a true encounter with Jesus Christ. When I really encounter who Jesus is, realizing that he is God, I immediately experience that I am not worthy to be with him. I am a sinner. A true encounter with God makes me feel my need, my sinfulness. I am not like God. I am not holy. I am not worthy to be with God.

Remember what happened on the day of Pentecost when Peter gave his first homily. He explained to his listeners the basic message of salvation. He told them who Jesus was and why he came: Jesus was the Messiah who died to save them. What was the result of Peter's incredible preaching?

> "When they heard this, they were cut to the heart, and they asked Peter and the other apos-

tles, 'What are we to do, my brothers?' Peter [said] to them, 'Repent and be baptized, every one of you, in the name of Jesus Christ for the forgiveness of your sins; and you will receive the gift of the holy Spirit.'" (Acts of the Apostles 2:37–38)

When the apostles want to summarize Jesus' message, they use the same words as Jesus: "This is the time of fulfillment. The kingdom of God is at hand. Repent, and believe in the gospel" (Mk 1:15). When I encounter the kingdom of God in Jesus, I have to reorder my life. It requires repentance. The Greek word for repentance is *metanoia*, which means to change one's mind or heart. It means turning away from my sinful way of life and turning toward God. This is what we always see in the Gospels. Those who truly encounter Jesus turn from their sinful ways and begin to follow him.

The third essential element of a true encounter happens at the very same moment that I realize I am a sinner. I also realize I am infinitely loved! Notice that when Simon Peter tells Jesus to depart from him, Jesus does not leave. In fact, Jesus draws Peter closer, saying, "Do not be afraid; from now on you will be catching men" (Lk 5:10).

Think of the woman caught in adultery in another scene in the Gospel. She knows that she is a sinner. As she stands before Jesus, after all her accusers have departed, he asks her, "Has no one condemned you?" (Jn

8:10). The Gospel continues: "She replied, 'No one, sir.' Then Jesus said, 'Neither do I condemn you. Go, [and] from now on do not sin anymore'" (v. 11). Whenever we really encounter Jesus, we encounter these two profound realities together. I am a sinner, but I am infinitely loved.

This reveals the depth of God's love for me, as Saint Paul says, "God proves his love for us in that while we were still sinners Christ died for us" (Rom 5:8). Pope Francis has written eloquently about how this truth of acknowledging I'm a sinner actually allows me to receive God's love more deeply: "I have often said that the place where my encounter with Jesus takes place is my sin. When you feel his merciful embrace, when you let yourself be embraced, when you are moved — that is when life can change."[3]

Finally, the fourth essential element of a real encounter: I am invited to follow Jesus in a new life. Someone who really encounters Jesus wants to be his disciple. They want to live as he lives and follow him. This is why the early disciples loved the title *Lord* for Jesus. It symbolized that he was the center of their lives. They belonged to him, and they began to center their lives on him. A real encounter leaves me changed, and I can't go on the way I lived before.

Paul is a powerful example of this, as we see the transformation he experienced after his encounter with Christ on the road to Damascus. When Saul met the Lord, he realized he had to reorder his whole life around Jesus. Years later he would describe the experience this way:

"Whatever gains I had, these I have come to consider a loss because of Christ. More than that, I even consider everything as a loss because of the supreme good of knowing Christ Jesus my Lord. For his sake I have accepted the loss of all things and I consider them so much rubbish, that I may gain Christ, and be found in him." (Philippians 3:7–9).

Have I encountered Jesus?

Everything begins with encounter. This is the first and most essential step in Christian faith. Without this encounter with Jesus, the truth of the Gospel will never make sense. The desire to grow in knowledge and understanding, the ability to come to know Jesus' truth and love, depends on encountering Jesus as the living God. Each of us must recognize that Jesus is God, that he knows me and loves me personally, and that he calls me to something more. And this encounter with Jesus deepens over time.

Mother Teresa was an Albanian nun who had been sent to Calcutta, India, as a missionary. After several years in religious life, she was on a train, traveling to her annual retreat, when she had an encounter with Jesus that changed her. She experienced Jesus on the cross, and he said, "I thirst." As we come to know Jesus better, he reveals himself more fully and shows us more deeply who we are. Mother Teresa was already a religious sister, but this deeper encounter changed her. She began to see that the purpose of her life was to satiate the thirst of Jesus on the cross by loving him in the poorest of the poor. She felt inspired to establish a religious community to accomplish this mission. The Missionaries of Charity is now one of the largest religious communities in the world, and Mother Teresa's sisters satiate the thirst of Jesus on every continent.

As Mother Teresa's life was coming to an end, her sisters asked her to write to them about this founding grace for their community, the encounter she had with Jesus' thirst. She began her explanation by reminding them that they, too, are called to the same kind of personal encounter with his love. She wrote:

I worry some of you still have not really met Jesus — one to one — you and Jesus alone. We may spend time in chapel — but have you seen with the eyes of your soul how he looks at you with love?

Do you really know the living Jesus — not from books, but from being with him in your heart? Have you heard the loving words he speaks to you? Ask for the grace, he is longing simply to give it. Until you can hear Jesus in the silence of your own heart, you will not be able to hear him saying "I thirst" in the hearts of the poor.

Never give up this intimate contact with Jesus as a real living person — not just an idea.

How can we last even one day living our life without hearing Jesus say "I love you" — impossible. Our soul needs that as much as the body needs to breathe the air. If not, prayer is dead — meditation only thinking.[4]

This letter is so striking because she was writing to her sisters. These were women who had given up family and homeland to live in voluntary poverty, chastity, and obedience for love of Jesus. Yet Mother Teresa says she worries some of them have not really met Jesus yet. If she can say that to her sisters, certainly we must ask ourselves if we have really met Jesus.

Have I met him one to one — I and Jesus alone? Have I heard Jesus speak to me in the silence of my own heart? Have I seen with the eyes of my heart how he looks at me with love? This is an encounter with a person. This is knowing Jesus as a living person.

In the Eucharist we have the opportunity to encounter Jesus in a profound and life-changing way. This is one of the reasons why Jesus remains with us in the Blessed Sacrament. In the Eucharist, he is present, here and now. He is here to share his love with us, to fill our hearts with his love. In the Eucharist Jesus gives us his Flesh and pours out his Blood for the life of the world — for my life and yours. And because Jesus Christ is truly here with us, our lives can be completely transformed.

Remember the disciples on the road to Emmaus in Luke 24? After seeing Jesus die, they are discouraged, and they decide to leave Jerusalem. The risen Lord draws near to them and begins to walk with them, but these disciples do not recognize him. In his compassion, he explains to them why the Messiah had to die so as to enter into his glory. As they reach their destination, their hearts are beginning to burn, and they cry out to him: "Stay with us, for it is nearly evening and the day is almost over" (Lk 24:29). Luke then says, "So he went in to stay with them. And it happened that, while he was with them at table, he took bread, said the blessing, broke it, and gave it to them. With that their eyes were opened and they recognized him, but he vanished from their sight" (vv. 29–31). Jesus did stay with them. He has stayed with us until today. He remains with us in the Eucharist. In the Eucharist we encounter the risen Lord who comes to share with us his very life, his very self. "For my flesh is true food, and my blood is true drink. Whoever eats my flesh and drinks my blood remains in me and I in him" (Jn 6:55–56).

At the heart of all the Church's profound teaching on the True Presence is this simple truth: The same Jesus who was born in Bethlehem, who walked on earth, who suffered and died on the cross, who rose from the dead and is seated at the right hand of the Father — this same Jesus is really, truly, and substantially present here and now in the Eucharist. He is here so you can receive him in holy Communion, so you can adore him in adoration. He is here so you can encounter him, and so he can speak to you and lead you into union with him.

Encountering Jesus in Eucharistic adoration

Adoration of the Blessed Sacrament is a powerful way to encounter Jesus. The Church has always argued that there is a personal presence of Jesus Christ in the Eucharistic Species. We are so convinced of this that when we come before the Eucharist, we give it the reverence due to God alone: We bend our knee. What looks like bread and wine has truly been transformed into the Body and Blood of Jesus.

When the priest stands at an altar and says, in the person of Christ, "This is my body. ... This is my blood ..." it actually happens. The bread and wine become the Body and Blood of Jesus, *sacramentally*. What does that mean? The appearance (meaning what it looks like, smells like, tastes like, etc.) doesn't change, but the substance — what it is — does change. Bread is no longer there. Wine is no longer there. What is there? Jesus. His Body, his Blood, his Soul, his Divinity — all that is Jesus is there.

This is the hallmark of Catholic belief in the Eucharist. Martin Luther, and many other Reformers, wanted to hold the Real Presence of Jesus in the Eucharist, but they did not believe in the actual change in the substance of the bread — the change we call *transubstantiation*. When asked if the consecrated Host was worthy of the same adoration due to God, every Reformer said no, while every Catholic always said yes. This is why Catholics and Orthodox reserve the Blessed Sacrament in a tabernacle, reverencing the living presence of God.

Adoration of the Blessed Sacrament as a practice

did not develop until the second millennium of Christianity, but even the early Church Fathers like Saint Augustine argued that an actual change in substance takes place, and that the sacrament is worthy of adoration. When Augustine was speaking about the disposition with which we must come to Communion, he said, "No one eats that flesh without first adoring it; we should sin were we not to adore it."[5]

This is why adoration is so powerful as an encounter with Jesus. Anyone who works with young people today knows this truth. Ask a young person who has a strong, vibrant faith how that came to be, and he or she will likely say something about Eucharistic adoration. I (Bishop Cozzens) have often seen this. Many years ago, I took a parish group to the Steubenville Youth Conference in St. Paul, Minnesota. One young man was not a very enthusiastic participant. His family was committed to the Faith, but he wasn't. Basically, his parents had required him to come.

When I saw him right before the evening adoration session, I felt inspired to challenge him. So, I got close to him, put my finger in his chest, and said: "Look out. God wants to do something powerful in your life tonight." At the end of the night, he came up to me with tears in his eyes and asked, "How did you know?" This young man had encountered Jesus, and it changed everything for him. He hardly ever missed a youth-group meeting after that.

As a young priest working in youth ministry, I often

saw this. Get young people to go to confession, give them a testimony about the reality and power of the personal love of Jesus Christ, and then put them in front of the Eucharist. Powerful things happen in adoration, because Jesus Christ is alive and really present in the Eucharist.

Of course, the most profound encounter we can have with the Lord is in the Mass. There we are invited not only to encounter his living presence, but to join in his sacrifice. We will see how this affects us in chapter 7. The celebration of the Eucharist in holy Mass is the "source and summit of the Christian life,"[6] and this is the place of the most transformative encounter.

Before we explore this, however, we need to look at the second pillar in the life of a Eucharistic missionary: Eucharistic Identity. Once we have encountered the living Jesus in the Eucharist, we begin to see how this reveals who we are. Our identity flows from the Eucharist, allowing us to live as Jesus lives, to share in his mission, and to bring him to others.

Questions to pray with and ponder

- What do you mean when you say, "I am a Christian"?
- Have you ever had a profound encounter with Jesus in Eucharistic adoration? If yes, what happened and what impact did it have in your life? If no, are you willing to ask for that grace?

CHAPTER 5
Eucharistic Identity

Identity is essential to mission. This was the insight we spoke about in the beginning of this book. Pope Leo XIII, seeing the struggle that would unfold between the enemy and God in the twentieth century, decided to focus his last major encyclical on the Eucharist, to strengthen the Church against the attacks of the enemy that would come. He believed that if Christians were strong in their Eucharistic faith, they would be strong against the temptations they would face.

The importance of identity can be seen in the life of the Lord Jesus himself. Just think about the beginning of his public ministry: He submits to be baptized on our behalf. As he comes up from the water, a voice from heaven says, "This is my beloved Son, with whom I am well pleased" (Mt 3:17). In this scene, his identity is revealed. Then he is led by the Spirit into the desert to be tempted by the devil. And how does the devil tempt

49

him? After he has fasted for forty days, the devil urges him, "If you are the Son of God, command that these stones become loaves of bread" (4:3). The enemy tempts him by attacking his identity.

One of the striking things about Jesus is that he never has an identity crisis. Jesus knows who he is, and he cannot be tempted. Earlier in his life, when he was only twelve years old, when his parents asked him why he stayed in Jerusalem to teach in the Temple, he responded simply, "Did you not know I must be in my Father's house?" (Lk 2:49). That "must" drives Jesus' whole life because he knows who he is as the beloved Son of the Father, and thus he desires only to do the Father's will. As he tells his followers, "I cannot do anything on my own; I judge as I hear, and my judgment is just, because I do not seek my own will but the will of the one who sent me" (Jn 5:30).

Relationship, Identity, and Mission

There is an essential principle, rooted in the Gospel, which is a paradigm for living the Christian life. The paradigm consists of three words: relationship, identity, and mission, often captured with the acronym RIM. This is the basic point: We were created by God for relationship, and from our relationships we know who we are — our identity. When we know who we are, then we know how we should act and what we should do — our mission. If we get the order wrong, then we end up being pulled away from our true identity into false identities.

The great temptation that happens to all of us is to take our identity from what we do — from our mission — not from the foundational relationships that reveal who we are. Often because of insecurities — lies we believe about ourselves — we find relationships difficult. We do not accept the truth of being loved unconditionally. So we look for our identity elsewhere, in what we do and in what others think of what we do. We try to prove to ourselves and others that we are good. This insecurity is the source of a lot of sin. When we live this way, we make *doing* more important than *being*, and we forget the truth that who we are is more important than what we do. Our hearts become restless because we are not resting in God's love.

It was Pope St. John Paul II who articulated this paradigm most clearly for the modern world. He pointed out in his Theology of the Body that we were made for communion (relationship), and that we discover the truth of who we are as we stand before the gaze of God. When I realize how God sees me, I discover that I was created by God, and I am loved unconditionally by him. Before I do anything, I am his beloved son or daughter. This identity is further developed as I stand before others and discover that I was made for others, that there is even within my body a need to give myself away. I was made for self-gift.

You may have noticed this truth in young people who come from good families. When children grow up in a family where they experience the deep security of being loved, they often have a natural self-confidence and are much less likely to look for love in the wrong places. They know who they are. Like someone who feels they are the son or daughter of a king, they will not settle for being drawn into things that are not worthy of them, and they don't feel the need to prove their identity by what they do.

It is love that reveals who we are. As John Paul II said in his first encyclical:

> Man cannot live without love. He remains a being that is incomprehensible for himself, his life is senseless, if love is not revealed to him, if he does not encounter love, if he does not experience it and make it his own, if he does not participate intimately in it.[1]

This is part of the problem of the world today — that so many people don't know this love.

We all need to have our identity refounded in Christ. John Paul II loved to quote the Second Vatican Council document *Gaudium et Spes*, which says, "Christ … fully reveals man to man himself."[2] When we encounter the truth of God's love in Jesus Christ, which we spoke about in the last chapter, we discover who we really are. It is then I discover that I, like Christ, am a beloved son or daughter of the Father. Yes, I am a son or daughter of the King.

John Paul II explains what a refounded identity

looks like:

> The man who wishes to understand himself thoroughly — and not just in accordance with immediate, partial, often superficial, and even illusory standards and measures of his being — he must with his unrest, uncertainty and even his weakness and sinfulness, with his life and death, draw near to Christ. He must, so to speak, enter into him with all his own self, he must "appropriate" and assimilate the whole of the reality of the Incarnation and Redemption in order to find himself. If this profound process takes place within him, he then bears fruit not only of adoration of God but also of deep wonder at himself.[3]

We experience a great unrest when we allow ourselves to be defined by superficial, illusory ideas that come from who the world tells us we are or need to be. Additionally, each of us experiences the depth of our own limitations, weakness, and sinfulness. All this creates self-doubt and great unrest in our hearts. John Paul II says the answer to our unrest is to draw near to Christ and begin to appropriate his identity — to understand ourselves in light of the love that Jesus Christ shows us. If we encounter his love and discover the truth that we have been redeemed, then we come to deep wonder, not only at the love of God, but at who he has made us to be.

Our identity is revealed in love.

This misunderstanding of our identity can also happen to the Church. The Church can lose her self-identity and forget that her relationship with the Trinity is the source of her life. This happens when people in the Church begin to live for mission instead of putting the primacy on relationship. This leads us to water down the Gospel, making it merely a self-help program or a means to helping others. Or it can lead to focusing too much on being professional and measuring metrics. It is important to be professional and seek even human ways to become effective in sharing the Gospel. But our mission should not be exclusively based on "what works." The real fire that changes hearts comes from the relationship we have with God, and if we are not first rooted in this, our ministry will be fruitless.

In his encyclical *Novo Millennio Inuente* ("At the Beginning of the New Millennium"), Pope St. John Paul II wrote that all our action must be rooted in contemplation. "It is important however that what we propose, with the help of God, should be profoundly rooted in contemplation and prayer. Ours is a time of continual movement which often leads to restlessness, with the risk of 'doing for the sake of doing.' We must resist this temptation by trying 'to be' before trying 'to do.'"[4] This is why "it is therefore essential that *education in prayer* should become in some way a key point of all pastoral planning."[5] And the high point of prayer is the liturgy, "the summit toward which the activity of the

Church is directed; at the same time it is the font from which all her power flows."[6]

Experiencing the truth of our identity in the Eucharist

This was one of the central points of the Second Vatican Council. For the Church, and for each member of the Church, our mission begins with our relationship with Christ, and the place we experience this relationship most profoundly is in the Eucharist. "The other sacraments, as well as with every ministry of the Church and every work of the apostolate, are tied together with the Eucharist and are directed toward it."[7] Every ministry, whether caring for the sick or the poor or sharing the good news; every apostolate, whether in the media or on college campuses; every work of the Church, is meant to be united with the Eucharist and directed toward it. The reason why we teach, why we feed the poor, why we evangelize, is to bring others to the Eucharist — to relationship with Jesus. Where do we find the strength to do these things? We find it in the Eucharist. The Church experiences her identity — who she is — in the Eucharist. And it is here where we as individuals also experience the truth of our identity. What does the Eucharist reveal to us about our identity?

First, it reveals that I am God's beloved. I am the bride for whom Jesus laid down his life. The Eucharist reveals to me how much I am loved, and it shows me my worth, my dignity. From Jesus: "This is my Body, which

will be given up for you ... this is the chalice of my Blood
... which will be poured out for you" (Eucharistic Prayer
II). Here I discover that I am worth dying for. Jesus gives
his body for me; he pours out his blood for me. As Paul
said, this should always be personal as well as communal: "I live by faith in the Son of God who has loved me
and has given himself up for me" (Gal 2:20).

Second, it reveals that I am the Body of Christ. This
is an ancient teaching of the Church on the Eucharist,
going back all the way to Saint Paul: "The cup of blessing that we bless, is it not a participation in the blood of
Christ? The bread that we break, is it not a participation
in the body of Christ? Because the loaf of bread is one,
we, though many, are one body, for we all partake of the
one loaf" (1 Cor 10:16–17). For Paul the reception of
communion is a covenantal act that brings about a real
union. We become the Body of Christ through our reception of the Eucharist because we become one with
Christ. This is true communally and even individually: "You are Christ's body, and individually parts of it"
(12:27).

This is where Saint Paul's whole theology of living
in Christ comes from. For Paul this truth means that I
become one with Jesus through baptism and the Eucharist, to the point that Christ lives his incarnation again
in me: "It is no longer I who live, but Christ who lives in
me" (RSV).

Here we see how our identity leads to mission. Since
we are the Body of Christ, this means we make Christ

present in the world today. He continues his mission in the world today through his body, which is the Church, and through each member of the Church. As the famous quote attributed to St. Teresa of Ávila expresses it: "Christ has no body now but yours. No hands, no feet on earth but yours. Yours are the eyes through which he looks with compassion on this world. Yours are the feet with which he walks to do good. Yours are the hands through which he blesses all the world." We have become one with Jesus through the Eucharist, and he wants to continue his presence in the world through each of us.

Yet even when we are trying to be good Christians, we are all prone to getting this principle — relationship, identity, mission — wrong. We easily place our mission above our relationship with Jesus, usually without realizing it. We feel valued when we are doing things for God, and we can be gradually tempted by the enemy to do so much that we become ineffective and burn out. It is far too easy to forget the words of Jesus, who puts the primacy on relationship:

> "Remain in me, as I remain in you. Just as a branch cannot bear fruit on its own unless it remains on the vine, so neither can you unless you remain in me. I am the vine, you are the branches. Whoever remains in me and I in him will bear much fruit, because without me you can do nothing." (John 15:4–5)

If we learn to remain in him, if we discover who we are from our relationship with Jesus, then we will be much more fruitful in living our mission. This leads us to the deeper understanding of what it means to live a Eucharistic life.

Questions to pray with and ponder

- How have you been tempted to view your worth in terms of what you *do*, rather than who you *are*? How can understanding the RIM paradigm (relationship > identity > mission) help reset your understanding of yourself and of God's plan for you?
- Do you believe you are called to be Jesus — in your family, in your workplace?
- How do you seek to live in union with Jesus? How might he be calling you to deeper union with him?

CHAPTER 6

Eucharistic Life, Part 1: Living in Communion

The Eucharist not only reveals who we are, but how we are to live. This is what the Church means by saying that the Eucharist is the "source and summit of the Christian life."[1] The Eucharist reveals to us what a Christian life looks like. In particular, the Eucharistic Sacrifice — the Mass — contains the very heart of the Christian life: Christ in his Paschal Mystery. (We will explore this in-depth in chapter 7.) In the Eucharist, Jesus Christ is given for us. Through our participation in the Eucharist, we are formed into the Body of Christ, and we learn to live as he lived.

Pope Benedict XVI spoke about this in his first encyclical, *Deus Caritas Est* ("God Is Love"). He wrote: "The Eucharist draws us into Jesus' act of self-oblation. More than just statically receiving the incarnate *Logos*, we enter into the very dynamic of his self-giving."[2] When we come to the Eucharist, we are not just before a static presence; rather, we are entering into a dynamic relationship with the One who has saved us and made us his own. Through this mystery, if we surrender to him, he forms us into his people, his body, and forms in us his own heart. He teaches us how to love as he loves in self-giving.

In this chapter and the next, we will focus on two central aspects of a Eucharistic life: communion and sacrifice. We have already spoken about some of the ramifications of Jesus' presence, the other important dimension of the Eucharistic mystery. In this chapter we will speak about communion, and in the next sacrifice, seeing how these two aspects allow us to live a fully Eucharistic life.

Called to communion

Since the earliest days of Christianity, the Eucharist has been the heart of the Christian community. This communion in the Lord through the Eucharist is meant to mark who we are as the Church. We see this in the Acts of the Apostles when it says, "They devoted themselves to the teaching of the apostles and to the communal life, to the breaking of the bread and to the prayers" (2:42). The "breaking of the bread" refers to the celebration of the Eucharist, the sacrament at the heart of their communal life. As Saint Paul went on his missionary journeys, he taught the communities he founded to celebrate the Eucharist. In one of the earliest texts of the New Testament, written just over twenty years after Christ's death, Paul says:

I received from the Lord what I also handed on to you, that the Lord Jesus, on the night he was handed over, took bread, and, after he had given thanks, broke it and said, "This is my body that is for you. Do this in remembrance of me." In the same way also the cup, after supper, saying, "This cup is the new covenant in my blood. Do this, as often as you drink it, in remembrance of me." For as often as you eat this bread and drink the cup, you proclaim the death of the Lord until he comes. (1 Corinthians 11:23–26)

Earlier in this same letter, Paul makes a very important point about a Eucharistic life and communion, pointing out to the Corinthians that their reception of the Eucharist makes them the Body of Christ: "We, though many, are one body, for we all partake of the one loaf" (10:17). Here, he chastises the Corinthian community because their sacramental communion is not being reflected in the way they love one another. They are not living like the Body of Christ they have received.

It seems that there is a division in the Christian community of Corinth between the rich and the poor. Thus, when the Corinthians share a meal after celebrating the Eucharist, "each one goes ahead with his own supper, and one goes hungry while another gets drunk" (1 Cor 11:21). They are not living as a real community; they are not sharing food between the rich and the poor, but rather are divided in selfishness. Paul points out in very strong terms that this kind of behavior is opposed to the Eucharist that they have just celebrated. It violates the communion.

In fact, he says if we receive Communion in this way, while in sinful violation of the Lord's commands, receiving holy Communion doesn't help us or make us holy. Instead, we eat and drink condemnation upon ourselves. He writes:

> Therefore whoever eats the bread or drinks the cup of the Lord unworthily will have to answer for the body and blood of the Lord. A person should examine himself, and so eat the bread and drink the cup. For anyone who eats and drinks without discerning the body, eats and drinks judgment on himself. That is why many among you are ill and infirm, and a considerable number are dying. If we discerned ourselves, we would not be under judgment; but since we are judged by [the] Lord, we are being disciplined so that we may not be condemned along with the world. Therefore, my brothers, when you come together to eat, wait for one another. (1 Corinthians 11:27–33)

Receiving holy Communion is a covenantal act. This is why we say "Amen," which is a covenantal word. To receive holy Communion is to say: "I want to live in this covenant with you. I want to live in communion with you,

Lord." This means I must also live in communion with the Church, Christ's Body.

If I choose to ignore this covenant, as Paul says the Corinthians are doing by not loving one another, then my reception of holy Communion actually hurts me. Paul says I will have to "answer for the body and blood of the Lord." This means I am in some way taking the responsibility of his death on myself. Note here the power of receiving holy Communion. Paul obviously believes the Eucharist is more than a symbol. He says if you receive it when you are not living correctly, in a state of sin, you eat and drink judgment upon yourself. He even says it will make you sick: "That is why many among you are ill and infirm, and a considerable number are dying" (v. 30). The Eucharist is supposed to be medicine, healing for our souls and bodies, but if we receive it unworthily, it does the opposite.

Here we see the Church's teaching about why we must be in a state of grace to receive holy Communion. But there are other ramifications. By receiving the Eucharist, I am dedicating myself to living in the communion of the Church which means loving the other members of the Church. Eucharistic communion is not just a personal act; I don't simply receive Jesus and draw close to Jesus. It also makes me a member of the Church, and I am called to live in loving communion as best as I can with the members of the Church. In fact, in the very next chapter of his First Letter to the Corinthians, Paul describes in detail what it means to say that the Church is the Body of

Christ and all of us are members of this Body. We become his body by eating his body and drinking his blood.

Love one another

In this way the Eucharist teaches us that we are not meant to live the Christian life alone. One of the places this truth is seen most clearly is in Jesus' Last Supper discourse in John's Gospel. Jesus tells his followers that he wants the members of his Church to love one another. "I give you a new commandment: love one another. As I have loved you, so you also should love one another. This is how all will know that you are my disciples, if you have love for one another" (Jn 13:34–35).

A Eucharistic life is a life lived in communion with our brothers and sisters in the Lord. It is a life in which we are able to form deep friendships because we share the same love: the love of Jesus Christ, who poured out his life for us. We have been filled with this love, and it burns in our hearts and is strengthened and nourished when we share it with others. When the Church is who she is supposed to be, she is a body beating with one heart, and all the members share her joy. This is a foretaste of heaven, where we will live in perfect communion with Christ and with one another. The Eucharist is meant to give us a foretaste of that experience of heaven.

Truth be told, we don't always experience Christian community as a foretaste of heaven. Many times, the Church community is a source of suffering for us. We are scandalized by the sins of leaders of the Church or other members of the body. We find it difficult to deal with people's weaknesses and character difficulties. It is normal to experience division and factions in our parishes. Not to mention our families, where we struggle with deep pains flowing from the ways we have hurt each other. What should the life of a Eucharistic missionary, a missionary of communion, look like in these painful circumstances? How does Christ call us to act?

Learning to love in these difficult situations in our families and parishes can be one of the most difficult things in the Christian life. Here is where our lives of personal prayer, which we will talk more about in the final chapter, become so important. We must learn to appropriate in our own hearts the love of the Eucharist. Living Eucharistic communion means learning to serve. It means learning to put others ahead of ourselves. It means learning to forgive.

One of the great examples of this is in John 13, where Jesus washes the feet of his disciples. It is noteworthy that the Gospel According to John does not contain the institution of the Eucharist at the Last Supper. John surely knew about the Eucharist, as he recorded the Bread of Life discourse of Jesus in chapter 6. Why did he leave it out of his Last Supper discourse? Many theorize that he was actually making a statement, because John's Gospel is also the only one that has the story of Jesus washing his disciples' feet. Of course, the master washing the disciples' feet was completely contrary to the culture of the time. Since the feet were the dirtiest part of the body, it was the job of the lowest servant to wash feet. Here we see the profundity of the image: Jesus empties himself and takes the form of a slave and pours out his blood on the cross to wash away our sins. He even washes the feet of Judas, who will betray him. He points out that this humble service is an example for us: "You call me 'teacher' and 'master,' and rightly so, for indeed I am. If I, therefore, the master and teacher, have washed your feet, you ought to wash one another's feet. I have given you a model to follow, so that as I have done for you, you should also do" (Jn 13:13–15).

A Eucharistic life demands that I learn how to wash the feet of those with whom I live in Eucharistic communion. How does this happen practically? When I am having some struggle with a person in my family or my parish, when I experience some hurt, can I learn to bring this before the Lord and tell him about the pain in my heart? Can I relate this suffering to him? Can I ask him how to see the situation and how I should respond? Our prayer lives are really meant to change our hearts. When I relate to him concrete struggles, Jesus can reveal the love of his heart. He can change my heart to become like his. He can teach me how he was able to wash the feet of Judas.

Have you ever tried spending a holy hour praying for someone you find difficulty loving? Have you gone to Mass during the week and placed them on the altar, asking God to change your heart toward them? This can be extremely difficult, and it involves real forgiveness, but the more I live in communion with Jesus through prayer and the sacraments, the more my heart becomes like his.

Friendship

A precious help to living in communion can be true Christian friends. Jesus called us his friends (see Jn 15:14), and where the love of Christ flourishes, friendship flourishes. We were never meant to live the Christian life alone. When we find others who share our desire to live a fully Eucharistic life, we should commit ourselves to supporting one another. This can be a great force for growing in holiness in our lives. Real friendship requires intentionality; it requires people who are committed to growing together. This requires vulnerability, accountability, and encouragement.

The word *vulnerability* comes from the Latin word *vulnus*, which means wound. To be vulnerable is to be willing to share one's wounds with another person. We see that Jesus was not ashamed of his wounds in the Resurrection, but even invited Thomas to touch them in his doubt (see Jn 20:27). As we learn to share our wounds with our brothers and sisters in Christ, gradually they, too, can become glorified wounds, like the wounds of Christ. Those places of hurt and need in our life can become places where we experience deep love. Being vulnerable at first is quite hard. It is not easy to admit my weakness and my need to my friend, or to ask for help. But if I do this in real friendship, it leads to real love, support, and communion.

Real friendship between Christians should also provide accountability. We need accountability to fulfill our commitments, especially in the Christian life. All of us fail at times to live the Eucharistic life we are called to live, and we need friends who will hold us accountable. Friendship strengthens us in our weakness. This is one of the reasons Jesus sent out his disciples two by two: So they could support and encourage one another when the mission got difficult; so they could remind each other to pray; so they could correct each other when they failed to be who they were called to be. Asking another to hold you accountable to your Christian way of life is humbling and requires vulnerability, but it also leads to great growth.

Finally, real friendship is a source of great encouragement. It is a great moment in a friendship when I experience that my friend sees my weakness and yet still chooses to be my friend. He or she believes in me deeper than my failure. My friend believes in my goodness and is there to help me get up and encourage me to start again. This is how Jesus related to Saint Peter after his betrayal. The Lord met Peter in his failure. He did not pretend it didn't happen, but in that moment, he asked him three times: "Do you love me?" (see Jn 21:15–17). The Lord encouraged and strengthened Peter by inviting him three times to affirm what he had three times denied. He gave him again the commission to be the leader of the Church, saying, "Feed my sheep." Peter realized he had failed, but he repented and received from the Lord encouragement to start over and begin anew.

To live a Eucharistic life is to live in real communion with other members of the Church. (Not everyone is experiencing this, right now, in their Christian life, but it is something that God desires.) If you don't have this kind of real Christian community, then ask God to help you find it. If you don't see it around you, begin to take concrete steps to build it. Start by inviting some friends to join a small group with you to study the Faith. There are many excellent small group studies available. Begin by sharing your faith and developing friendships. This can lead to the deeper communion God desires. Some people find these kind of relationships through online Christian communities like the one we are trying to form of Eucharistic Missionaries. We cannot live a truly Eucharistic life alone. We need friends. If you don't already have some close friends who are also seeking to live their life in the Lord — friends who offer you real vulnerability, accountability, and encouragement — God will help you to find those friends. This will be a great strength to living a Eucharistic life in communion.

The miracle of Eucharistic communion

Eucharistic communion can change our hearts and make us able to love like Christ. We see a great example of this in the shrine of St. Maria Goretti in Nettuno, Italy. At eleven years old, Maria Goretti was murdered by a hired hand on her family farm, who was attempting to seduce and rape her. Alessandro Serenelli went to jail for twenty-seven years for stabbing Maria to death. While he was in prison, Maria appeared to him and told him she wanted him to be in heaven with her. He underwent a profound conversion and did many years of penance.

When he was released from prison, Alessandro went to Maria's mother, Assunta Goretti, to beg her forgiveness, which she gave him. She had heard Maria herself forgive Alessandro on her deathbed. At the shrine there is a photograph of the two of them kneeling next to each other at the communion rail to receive Communion together at Midnight Mass on Christmas. Here is the miracle of Eucharistic communion: It can change our hearts so much that we can forgive even those who have deeply hurt us. Let us pray that we might be true missionaries of this Eucharistic communion.

Questions to pray with and ponder

- What aspects of living in communion with others do you find most challenging? Most rewarding?
- Is the Lord calling you to wash the feet of any people in your life? Who are they?
- Do you have friends with whom you can be vulnerable and accountable as you seek to live a Eucharistic life? If yes, who are they? Take a moment to thank God for them. If no, pray that God will help you find such friends, and keep your eyes open for opportunities he will provide to meet them.

CHAPTER 7

Eucharistic Life, Part 2: Living Sacrificially

It is impossible to live a Eucharistic life without sacrifice, because the Eucharist is a sacrifice. We often forget the sacrificial aspect of the Eucharist, but it is extremely important to really understanding a Eucharistic life.

The word *sacrifice* literally means to make something holy — in Latin, *sacrum* + *facere*. To make a sacrifice is to make an offering to God. It is very connected to worship, where we give God what he is due by giving him ourselves. The supreme sacrifice is the sacrifice of Jesus on the cross. But Jesus invites us to take up our cross and follow him. This means we, too, must learn to embrace suffering as a way of self-gift. When we add love to our pain, difficulties, or struggles, they become a sacrifice. This is what the Eucharist wants to form in us, and it is at the heart of being a Eucharistic missionary.

Consider Jesus' mission. What was his greatest act? It was not healing the man born blind, feeding thousands, or even raising the dead. No, it was the self-gift of his passion, which gives life to the world. This is the act that redeems us. As Jesus says, "Unless a grain of wheat falls to the ground and dies, it remains just a grain of wheat; but if it dies, it produces much fruit" (Jn 12:24). This principle is seen in the lives of all the saints, and we must live it as well if we want ours to be a truly Eucharistic life. If we want to bear fruit for Jesus as missionaries, we must be willing to make a gift of our lives for and with him.

This is the true heart of what it means to live a Eucharistic life. Self-gift is the way of life the Eucharist wants to form in us. Mother Teresa said it this way, shared in a video at the 18th Annual National Catholic Prayer Breakfast, March 14, 2023: "We need to be woven with the Eucharist, we need that oneness, we need to become so one with Jesus that we can be also broken, that the people can eat us, that we can be really spent like Jesus spent himself. That is why Jesus made himself the bread of life."

In this chapter, we will ponder the truth of the Sacrifice of the Mass and how we are called to live this sacrifice every day — how we must let ourselves be broken with the Eucharist.

"Do this in memory of me"
In the Mass, Jesus makes his sacrifice on the cross pres-

ent to us. The Jewish people already had an understanding in Jesus' time that, when they celebrated the Passover, that salvific event, which happened once, was made present anew. The Passover is a memorial, a ritual in which the Jewish people make memory of the event that made them God's people: the Exodus and the covenant at Mount Sinai. However, for them this remembering is not simply a calling to mind. They believe that the saving effects of that event, which happened thousands of years before, are actually made present when they celebrate the Passover. As the Jewish Haggadah prayers say, prayers which are still recited in Jewish families at the Passover meal: "We, today, are saved from the Egyptians. … We, today, are entering our inheritance."[1] The modern Jew can say "I was" or "we were" saved from slavery in Egypt, not because he had been there, but because he had celebrated the event and in this way really participated. The Haggadah celebration says, "Every Jew must consider oneself as having come out of Egypt."[2]

Jesus is speaking into this understanding when he says to his apostles, "Do this in memory of me." They would come to understand that they were to make a memorial of this celebration, and this memorial is not merely remembering; it truly makes the saving event of Jesus' Paschal Mystery present to us. The event by which he saves us from sin and forms us as his people.

To understand this, it is important to understand exactly what is happening on the cross. Jesus on the cross is fundamentally an act of worship. It is a sacrificial offering of the Son to the Father for the salvation of the world. In fact, it is the only true act of worship that has ever been offered in the history of the world. Jesus, who is both fully divine and fully human, offers himself to the Father for our salvation. This is the sacrifice that is actually able to repair, for all, the sins of the world. The Old Testament sacrificial system was merely a foreshadowing of this sacrifice.

This is why the New Testament makes clear that Jesus' death fulfilled the Old Testament. When Jesus died on the cross, the veil of the Temple, which marked off the Holy of Holies where the high priest offered yearly sacrifice in atonement for the sins of the people, was torn in two (see Mt 27:51; Mk 15:38; Lk 23:45). When Jesus died on the cross, he entered the true Holy of Holies, says the book of Hebrews: "He entered once for all into the sanctuary, not with the blood of goats and calves but with his own blood, thus obtaining eternal redemption" (9:12). And his blood "speaks more eloquently than that of Abel" (12:24). What did Abel's blood say? It cried out for vengeance (Gn 4:10). What does the blood of Jesus say? It cries out for mercy.

The cross, then, is the true act of worship, the fulfillment of all the worship of the Old Testament, that redeems us from sin and death. And Christ gives this worship an enduring presence in the Eucharist. The Mass re-presents his sacrifice here and now. Pope Francis makes this clear in *Desiderio Desideravi*:

The content of the bread broken is the cross of
Jesus, his sacrifice of obedience out of love for
the Father. If we had not had the Last Supper,
that is to say, if we had not had the ritual an-
ticipation of his death, we would have never
been able to grasp how the carrying out of his
being condemned to death could have been in
fact *the* act of perfect worship, pleasing to the
Father, the only true act of worship, the only
true liturgy.[3]

The words of Jesus at the Last Supper represent the
heart of the Eucharist, and they are intimately connected with Jesus' death on the cross. At every Mass,
we hear these words spoken again by the priest: "This
is my Body, which will be given up for you. ... This is
the chalice of my Blood, the Blood of the new and eternal covenant, which will be poured out for you and for
many for the forgiveness of sins. Do this in memory of
me." The words of Jesus and his death are essentially in-
terdependent. The words without the death would have
no meaning. In fact, the words reveal that his death is
actually a gift of his life for us, an act of self-giving love.

These three things are intimately connected: The
words of institution at the Last Supper, Jesus' death on the
cross, and his resurrection. We call these three together
the Paschal Mystery of Jesus, made present every time
we celebrate the Eucharist; suffering and death are transformed into life, by the love which is stronger than death.

The *Catechism of the Catholic Church* states it this way:

> In the liturgy of the Church, it is principally his own Paschal mystery that Christ signifies and makes present. ... His Paschal mystery is a real event that occurred in our history, but it is unique: all other historical events happen once, and then they pass away, swallowed up in the past. The Paschal mystery of Christ, by contrast, cannot remain only in the past, because by his death he destroyed death, and all that Christ is — all that he did and suffered for all men — participates in the divine eternity, and so transcends all times while being made present in them all. The event of the Cross and Resurrection *abides* and draws everything toward life. (1085)

It is clear that the Eucharist is so much more than just a meal. It is the act of perfect worship, re-presenting the death and resurrection of Jesus through the priest, who stands in the person of Christ.

Making our lives true worship

Why does Christ make his Paschal Mystery present in the Eucharist? He does this so that we, too, can offer true worship. He wants us to learn to live the Paschal Mystery, making a gift of our lives in imitation of him.

Jesus says to his apostles, "Do this in memory of me." He certainly intends for them and their successors to imitate this ritual, as we saw the early Church begin to do right away. But the command to "do this in memory of me" should also have a deeper meaning for us. It means: "Do for me what I have done for you. Offer my sacrifice again by means of these visible signs of bread and wine, and by the grace it gives you, live this sacrifice in your lives, making yourselves a living sacrifice. Learn to bring your sufferings, your crosses, to this altar to offer them to the Father with me."

Here is the key to understanding the Eucharist: It is meant to teach us how to transform our lives, especially the suffering of our lives, into a gift. If we learn this lesson, we learn how to offer our lives through, with, and in Christ as his true missionaries. Pope Benedict XVI stated this beautifully in his apostolic exhortation on the Eucharist:

> Christians, in all their actions, are called to offer true worship to God. Here the intrinsically Eucharistic nature of Christian life begins to take shape. The Eucharist, since it embraces the concrete, everyday existence of the believer, makes possible, day by day, the progressive transfiguration of all those called by grace to reflect the image of the Son of God (cf. Rom 8:29ff.). There is nothing authentically human — our thoughts and affections, our words and

> deeds — that does not find in the sacrament of
> the Eucharist the form it needs to be lived to
> the full.[4]

One of the mysteries of the Christian life is that Jesus does not take away suffering. Jesus comes to redeem us, but he does not end suffering. Rather he enters into suffering and transforms it. He makes suffering a way of love, the way that he redeems us.

We all have suffering in our lives. It is unavoidable, and Jesus promised it would be so. He told us we must take up our cross and follow him. Normally, suffering turns us in on ourselves and isolates us from others. This is the natural reaction to suffering — it leads to anger, fear, or sadness. But Jesus wants to teach us how to transform our suffering as he did. He wants to teach us the value of suffering, the gift of the cross in our lives. He wants to teach us that suffering can be a great force for good in the world, when we learn to unite that suffering to the offering of Jesus. In this way suffering becomes valuable and not empty; it is part of the redemption of the world. This is what we hear in the Second Letter to Timothy: "Bear your share of hardship for the gospel with the strength that comes from God" (1:8). The person who lives a Eucharistic life learns the value of suffering.

How does this happen practically? When I am experiencing some pain, some distress, some suffering — anything from a minor annoyance to a major tragedy, or even the suffering of my own sinfulness — in my imagination, I should think of some need to which I want to apply this suffering. It can be anything: the evil of abortion, a young person I know who is struggling, my own sanctification. I can even leave the need up to Jesus or Mary to decide. Then, I ask Jesus to take this suffering and unite it to his own, and to apply the merits to the need for which I'm offering it.

This is the famous Catholic teaching of "offering it up." It is really a profound way to stop us from turning in on ourselves in our suffering and wallowing in our pain. Offering it up allows us to use the energy of love to transform suffering. Suffering wants to turn us in on ourselves; love gives us the energy to transform suffering into self-gift.

The saints learn this lesson well. A practical example of this is found in the life of Elisabeth Leseur, a French woman who lived at the end of the nineteenth century and whose cause is open for canonization. Her husband was an atheist, and his questioning of the Faith actually led her to deepen her own. She prayed daily for his conversion and tried to witness true love and generosity to him. In 1907 she began a long battle with poor health, and she died of cancer in 1917. She offered her suffering for the conversion of others, especially her husband. This teaching on "offering it up" transformed her whole life into an offering of love. She wrote in her spiritual diary:

> We pray, suffer, and labor in ignorance of the consequence of our acts and prayers. God

makes them serve his supreme plan; gradually they take their effect, winning one soul, then another. They hasten the coming of the kingdom of God, and by the other beings, acts, and desires they give birth to ... they will exert an influence that will endure until the end of time.[5]

After Elizabeth died her husband found her diary and was converted to the Catholic Faith by reading it. He even became a Dominican priest. Elizabeth lived a Eucharistic life.

Of course, it would be a fantasy to think that my fasting or other suffering on its own can help other people change or endure their own suffering. But this is not just about me. Through the power of our baptismal priesthood, we are able to unite our offering to the offering of Christ, asking him to apply some of the infinite merits of his sacrifice to the needs we are praying for. This is no mere fantasy; it is living the power of the cross in our lives.

This is what Paul is talking about when he says, "In my flesh I am filling up what is lacking in the afflictions of Christ on behalf of his body, which is the Church" (Col 1:24). What is lacking in Christ's affliction? What is lacking is the sufferings we, his body, undergo today. Those sufferings are still waiting to be offered to the Father for the redemption of the world. Thus we can cooperate in Jesus' work of redemption.

This is particularly connected to what Our Lady

was doing at the foot of the cross. Mary was not there as a spectator. No, she was actively participating in the cross. She was offering a sacrifice, too. She consented to the death of her son, which caused a sword to pierce her own heart. She suffered so acutely that the Fathers of the Church called her a martyr. She offered her own life with her son's. At the foot of the cross, Mary could see what was going on invisibly behind the visible reality. She could see the sacrament. The outward sign was the death of an innocent man, but the inward reality was the Son of God offering himself for the redemption of the world. And so Mary offered herself with him. She cooperated in redemption through her own offering, uniting her suffering to his. Mary was exercising her priesthood there — her royal priesthood in which all Christians share.

Active participation

This is how we are meant to be present at Mass — not as a mere spectators, but, like Mary, making our own offering, uniting our offering to Christ's offering for the salvation of the world. We say yes to his sacrifice with our own life.

This is also what Vatican II meant by active participation in the liturgy. What is active participation? Pope Benedict points out that it is not to be understood in an external way. Active participation is not simply doing external things — standing, kneeling, sitting, singing, reading, etc. Active participation is primarily about self-gift. Pope Benedict XVI wrote:

The active participation called for by the council must be understood in more substantial terms, on the basis of a greater awareness of the mystery being celebrated and its relationship to daily life. The conciliar constitution *Sacrosanctum Concilium* encouraged the faithful to take part in the Eucharistic liturgy not "as strangers or silent spectators," but as participants "in the sacred action, conscious of what they are doing, actively and devoutly."... This exhortation has lost none of its force. The council went on to say that the faithful "should be instructed by God's word, and nourished at the table of the Lord's Body. They should give thanks to God. Offering the immaculate Victim, not only through the hands of the priest but also together with him, they should learn to make an offering of themselves. Through Christ, the Mediator, they should be drawn day by day into ever more perfect union with God and each other."[6]

At Mass the priest says, "Pray brothers and sisters that my sacrifice and yours may be acceptable to God the Almighty Father." What is our sacrifice? It is our sufferings, our struggles, which we bring and place on the altar. By virtue of our baptism, all of us share in the priesthood of Christ, and we can unite our sufferings with his. This is active participation where, together with the ordained priest, they "learn to make an offering of themselves."

This is also connected to what Vatican II means when it talks about the Eucharist as the "source and summit" of the Christian life: "Taking part in the Eucharistic Sacrifice, which is the source and summit [some translations use fount and apex as terms here] of the whole Christian life, they offer the Divine Victim to God, and offer themselves along with It."[7] The Eucharistic Sacrifice is the source of our life because it fills us with Christ's divine life. It is the summit of our life because it allows us to bring our lives to the altar and make a true gift to the Father in worship.

Indeed, as Vatican II also teaches:

> The Most Blessed Eucharist contains the entire spiritual boon of the Church, that is, Christ himself, our Pasch and Living Bread, by the action of the Holy Spirit through his very flesh vital and vitalizing, giving life to men who are thus invited and encouraged to offer themselves, their labors and all created things, together with him. In this light, the Eucharist shows itself as the source and the apex of the whole work of preaching the Gospel.[8]

This is in fact the plan of Jesus for the healing of our world. The Eucharist is at the heart of that plan because, through the Mass, we are able to participate in Christ's transformation of the world. We can take our sufferings and make them an offering.

These sufferings that we offer can include our weaknesses, and even our failures and sins when we repent. Perhaps we suffer because we are anxious, sensitive, or attached to earthly things, or we don't trust enough. We sin because we struggle with a habit we are trying to overcome. It doesn't matter the source of our suffering, whether it is from outside circumstances beyond our control, or from our own weakness or even our sin. These sufferings can still be brought to Christ's sacrifice and offered to him.

The famous Carmelite priest Wilfrid Stinissen points out that we should be willing to offer our weakness and even our sadness about our failures to Christ in the Eucharist:

> A great deal would happen in our lives if every time we celebrated the Eucharist we would place on the paten something of our own, something that we know is directed wrongly and therefore blocks us. ... We imagine all too often that we must offer beautiful things to God. But the beautiful does not need to be offered to God. It is already in God's sphere. It is the evil, that which has not yet found its right place, that must be lifted up and placed there, where it belongs, in God's radiance.[9]

Suffering and mission

Saint Paul understood the importance of suffering for

his mission. He explains how it is his own living of the Paschal Mystery that makes his mission fruitful:

> But we hold this treasure in earthen vessels, that the surpassing power may be of God and not from us. We are afflicted in every way, but not constrained; perplexed, but not driven to despair; persecuted, but not abandoned; struck down, but not destroyed; always carrying about in the body the dying of Jesus, so that the life of Jesus may also be manifested in our body. For we who live are constantly being given up to death for the sake of Jesus, so that the life of Jesus may be manifested in our mortal flesh. So death is at work in us, but life in you. (2 Corinthians 4:7–11)

Paul saw his affliction — his being perplexed, his persecution, his being struck down — as his participation in Christ's Paschal Mystery. It was Jesus dying in him! And this was fruitful for his mission, as he tells the Corinthians: "So death is at work in us, but life in you" (2 Cor 4:12).

This is what the Eucharist teaches us. Through the re-presentation of Christ's sacrifice at the Mass, we can see our own lives in light of the Paschal Mystery, and we are meant to learn how our own suffering is central to the mission God has given us. This is the true heart of a Eucharistic missionary.

As a young priest, I (Bishop Cozzens) was sent to

study in Rome during the final years of the pontificate of Pope St. John Paul II. In October 2004, about six months before John Paul II died, I attended a beatification Mass in St. Peter's Square. The pope was presiding at the ceremony, but he was too weak at that point in his life to celebrate Mass publicly. He presided from his chair over the Liturgy of the Word and preached the homily, but then one of the cardinals went to the altar to preside at the Eucharistic prayer. I was privileged to be selected to distribute holy Communion, so I was standing just about ten feet behind the cardinal, holding a ciborium full of hosts. And there was no one between me and John Paul II, who was just to my left about twenty yards away. The pope was sitting, but when the time came for the consecration, he turned to the master of ceremonies on his right and motioned with his hand that he wanted help to kneel at the kneeler in front of him. The master of ceremonies put his hand on his shoulder as if to say, "Holy Father, it is OK, you can sit during the consecration." But John Paul II pushed the hand away and pointed again to the kneeler. He was insistent. He wanted to kneel! So, two men lifted him up out of his chair and with great labor placed him down on his knees on the kneeler. I watched his face closely during the entire Eucharistic prayer. I felt like I was seeing Jesus on the cross — he was clearly in agony — yet he wanted to kneel.

It seemed very clear to me that Pope John Paul II was living the mystery of the Eucharist in his own body. I could see on his face that, as Jesus was being offered on the altar, he, too, was offering his own life, with Jesus, for the salvation of the world. As Jesus' body and blood were being given and poured out at the Mass, he, too, was pouring out all his strength, all his life with Jesus. It was as if Jesus was living his passion again before my eyes, in the body of Saint John Paul II.

This is an icon of what it means to live a Eucharistic life. It means I want my life to be an offering, a gift, just as Pope St. John Paul II did at that Eucharist and in his whole life. This is what the Eucharist wants to form in us.

Jesus wants to live his sacrifice again, in your heart and mine. Will you let him? Will you follow the invitation of Paul to Timothy, to "bear your share of hardship for the Gospel with the strength that comes from God" (2 Tm 1:8)? If you will do this, then Christ can make your mission fruitful. Then you will be able to say, with Saint Paul, "Death is at work in us, but life in you." Then you will be sharing in the Eucharistic mission Christ gave us.

Questions to pray with and ponder

- What crosses are you carrying in your life right now? What would it look like for you to offer them as a sacrifice, in union with Jesus' sacrifice?
- How are sacrifice and mission related? Why is sacrifice so important if we want our mission in Christ to be fruitful?

CHAPTER 8

Eucharistic Mission

In this journey to becoming a Eucharistic mission-ary, we have considered how Eucharistic Encounter leads to a profound sense of Eucharistic Identity, which leads us to Eucharistic Life, of communion and sacrifice. Now we arrive at the final pillar of being a Eucharistic missionary: adopting the Eucharistic Mission.

It can be easy for us to see the Eucharist and mission as two separate realities. The Eucharist is about prayer, the interior life, and encounter. We receive Jesus in the Eucharist at Mass and spend time with him in adoration. We think of the mission of the Church as separate, though perhaps distantly related. The Church's mission is a more active venture, including everything that the Church does "out there," whether evangelizing or promoting the common good.

An authentically Catholic worldview, however, cannot accept that bifurcation of Eucharist and mission. These are not two distinct concepts. The Eucharist is the heart of the Church's mission, its source and summit. And mission is not an accidental quality, but essential to the reception of Jesus in the Eucharist. In every Mass, Jesus himself goes on mission, rushing down to the altar, to accomplish some definite purpose. Therefore, the final step in becoming a Eucharistic missionary is to make his purpose in becoming the bread of life ours.

It can be strange for us as Catholics to think of the Eucharist as having a mission, because we are still often caught in the trap of thinking of the Eucharist as a *what* rather than a *who*. Jesus is really substantially present in the Eucharist, so it is truly a who. And every *who* has something that drives them. We are driven by desires, often very deep ones, that compel us to action. The same is true of Jesus in the Eucharist. He is driven by the desire to complete his mission. We unpacked in chapter 3 how Jesus was sent by the Father to bring his children home. That mission is extended to every person, in every time and every place. We do not live in first-century Judea. Thousands of years later, what Jesus came to accomplish has to reach each of us. With every available option in front of him, and with the wisdom that comes from being the all-knowing and all-powerful Lord of the Universe, Jesus decided to ensure that his mission would continue even after he returned to the Father by establishing a Church.

Jesus is on a mission

We get so used to hearing the Gospel every Sunday that we can lose sight of what's happening there. If we read it with fresh eyes, the person of Jesus almost pops off the page, and his "words and deeds"[1] are filled with incredible dynamism and energy. Jesus is moving, energetic. He is going somewhere, and *fast.*

This is because Jesus is on a mission. Consider the very beginning of Mark's Gospel. Barely a dozen verses have passed before Jesus has been baptized and gone into the desert. There, we know from Luke, he contends with the temptations of the devil, and when he returns to Galilee, he announces: "This is the time of fulfillment. The kingdom of God is at hand. Repent, and believe in the gospel" (Mk 1:15).

This contextualizes everything. Why is Jesus baptizing, teaching, healing, sending out his disciples, raising Lazarus from the dead? He has come to establish a kingdom. This is his mission. Everything that will follow — his public ministry; his teaching; his gathering of apostles and disciples; his passion, death, and resurrection; all of Church history — all of it, ultimately, is about Jesus' campaign to establish his kingdom.

This helps us understand an interesting, potentially even awkward, exchange between the apostles and Jesus in the Acts of the Apostles. Jesus, having risen from the dead weeks earlier, takes his closest followers up to a hill called Olivet, outside of Jerusalem. Then, "When they had gathered together they asked him, 'Lord, are you at this time going to restore the kingdom to Israel?'" (Acts 1:6). This question is striking. Forty days earlier, Jesus rose from the dead. Since then, he had continued to gather with them, proving that he was truly risen. He met Peter by the Sea of Galilee and forgave him for his denial. He had Thomas touch his wounds and healed his doubt. He walked with the disciples going to Emmaus and made himself known to them in the breaking of the bread. What more could they want?

But we read in Acts 1:3 why they are still confused. For forty days, Jesus has been talking to them about the kingdom of God. They have observed marvels, for he is risen, indeed. But they still do not see the kingdom he is talking about.

Jesus apparently rebuffs their question at first. He says to them, "It is not for you to know times and seasons which the Father has appointed by his own authority" (v. 7). Yet it is not really a rebuff. They are asking him a when question: "Lord, are you at *this time* …" (v. 6). In response, he essentially says to them, "I won't tell you when, but I will tell you who." He tells them: "*You* will receive power when the Holy Spirit comes upon you, and you will be my witnesses in Jerusalem, Judea, Samaria, and to the ends of the earth" (v. 8, emphasis added).

This is what the Church is. Jesus has rescued us from the kingdom of darkness and brought us home to the Father's house, the kingdom of God. But this entrance into the Kingdom and the possibility of a new life to be found there does not have to wait until heaven. We can begin to experience it now, here, today, in the communion of the Catholic Church.

Jesus did not become incarnate, suffer, die, and rise to form an elite club for religiously inclined people. He did so to save us, and he established a Church to continue his mission. For the last two thousand years, the Catholic Church has been sent *urgently* to extend the rescue mission of Jesus Christ to every person, in every time and every place. The Church does much, teaches much, celebrates much, practices much, but every smell, bell, rosary, and statue exists for a single purpose, as Pope St. Paul VI says in *Evangelii Nuntiandi*, "to evangelize."

We do not invent our own purpose or decide what our mission is. It has been given to us by Jesus, who was sent from the Father. "As the Father has sent me, so I send you" (Jn 20:21). We have been given, in the sacramental economy of the Catholic Church, the answer to every question and longing of the human heart. Where Adam and Eve once lost the life they had been given with a meal, Jesus now restores it — once again, in a meal.

This is the mission of Jesus in the Eucharist. He is still here to bring life, and not just to those who already know about this life. He wants to bring it to every person. This means that the Church in every age should organize herself around the question of how to accomplish this mission most effectively.

The mission is urgent
Today, the Church often seems to have lost the sense of

this mandate. Both as an institution and as individuals, we tend to sideline our mission. Yet we live in a time in which this mission has never been more urgent.

After Pentecost, when the apostles received power as Jesus had told them they would, they exploded out of the Upper Room. The early Church was constantly pressed and persecuted by the powers of the day, but the Christians' witness — particularly their martyrdom — was so compelling that much of the ancient world came to be baptized in a matter of centuries.

The Church grew almost inexplicably quickly, baptizing not just people but cultures as well, and this significantly changes the overall tone of the Church's life.

Over the last two millenia, there have been two overarching contexts or situations in which the Church has lived out her life and mission in the world. First is the missionary context in which the apostles were originally engaged. Pope St. John Paul II described this work this way in *Redemptoris Missio*:

> Missionary activity proper, namely the mission *ad gentes*, is directed to "peoples or groups who do not yet believe in Christ," "who are far from Christ," in whom the Church "has not yet taken root," and whose culture has not yet been influenced by the Gospel. It is distinct from other ecclesial activities inasmuch as it is addressed to groups and settings which are non-Christian because the preaching of the Gospel and

the presence of the Church are either absent or insufficient. It can thus be characterized as the work of proclaiming Christ and his Gospel, building up the local Church and promoting the values of the Kingdom. The specific nature of this mission *ad gentes* consists in its being addressed to "non-Christians."[2]

The Church has always continued this missionary work in places not yet deeply suffused by the Gospel.

However, slowly, as the majority of folks become Christian in a given culture and the Christian worldview begins to shape not just the life of the Church but "secular" life as well, the context of the Church's life changes quite a bit. The work of the Church does not become so much evangelizing as it is taking care of and organizing the life of faithful Catholics, what we call "pastoral care." This second cultural context in which the Church carries out her life and mission has been called by some "Christendom."

For centuries, in the Western world, Christianity was the cultural context in which people lived and the dominant lens that shaped how they saw. Whether they practiced the Faith or not, people typically shared a way of viewing the world that had been significantly influenced by the Christian worldview. In these cultures, the Church's dominant mode of operating became almost exclusively that of pastoral care. Largely, faithful people needed to be given the sacraments, have their kids educated in the Faith, and be encouraged to persevere toward holiness. The broader culture shared the same Christian worldview, and many secular institutions openly supported the work of the Church. Evangelization, or the work of mission, becomes something that happens "out there" somewhere, in faraway lands, and is not something with which the daily activity of the Church is necessarily concerned.

Today, we no longer live in a Christian culture. Pope Francis has put it this way, "We are living, not just in an age of change, but in a change of age." It was Venerable Fulton Sheen who said, at a conference in 1974: "We are at the end of Christendom. Not of Christianity, not of the Church, but of Christendom. Now what is meant by Christendom? Christendom is economic, political, social life as inspired by Christian principles. That is ending — we've seen it die."

God has chosen us to live in a moment in the history of the world in which much will be needed from us as Catholics. We no longer live in Christendom, even as we retain some of its structures, habits, and ways of thinking; rather, our age more closely resembles the missional context in which the apostles preached. This should not be a cause for despair, however, but a rallying cry for us. In fact, Fulton Sheen ended the above quote with this encouragement: "These are great and wonderful days in which to be alive."

In the face of this cultural reality, we have many choices. We can choose to fight, to become combative and pick sides. Or we can choose flight, running for the hills and battening down the hatches. Or we can freeze, do nothing, because we do not see what can be done in the face of such overwhelming odds. Or, like the apostles, we can remember our identity as Church. We can go on mission again.

If we are living in a missionary context, then the only option is for the Church to not just try to pretend that we still live in Christendom, but to respond by conforming our life to this context. We should study what the apostles did and imitate their example. We should look for images of what the Church on mission looks like in the centuries of the Church's effective mission *ad gentes* and begin to try to shape our reality to look how theirs looked.

If we are to live Eucharistic Mission, we have to make the mission of Jesus in the Eucharist — to bring life to the full to every person, in every time, and every place — our mission. Today, the Church as a whole, and each of us as individual members of the Body of Christ, needs to undergo a missionary conversion so we can set about this important work.

Conversion and *transformation* are nice words. But what we mean by them is change, and change is hard. This missionary conversion will not be easy, yet, again, we find our hope in the Eucharist. The Eucharist is both the source and summit of this missionary conversion. In *Desiderio Desideravi*, Pope Francis wrote:

The world still does not know it, but everyone is invited to the supper of the wedding of the Lamb (Rv 19:9). ... We must not allow ourselves even a moment of rest, knowing that still not everyone has received an invitation to this supper or knowing that others have forgotten it or have got lost along the way in the twists and turns of human living. This is what I spoke of when I said, "I dream of a 'missionary option,' that is, a missionary impulse capable of transforming everything, so that the Church's customs, ways of doing things, times and schedules, language and structures can be suitably channeled for the evangelization of today's world rather than for her self-preservation" (*Evangelii Gaudium*, n. 27). I want this so that all can be seated at the supper of the sacrifice of the Lamb and live from him.[3]

It is the love of God, which we receive in the Eucharist, that gives each member of the Church the energy and desire for mission. And it is the love of God, which we receive in the Eucharist, to which we are inviting those to whom we go.

God has a plan for how he will bring the entire world back to himself. He is already on the move, at work, pressing into our world to bring each and every human heart the life to the full it was made for. And in this drama, each of us has a definitive part to play. In some part of this drama, *you* are God's plan A. God has planned for *you* to help him reach certain people, eternal souls for whom he is desperately searching. God has chosen *you* to be the balm for some wound, whether it be a societal ill, a broken pattern of human living, or individual hurts and broken hearts. God has placed in *your* mind and heart specific projects and initiatives for the restoration of all creation in Christ Jesus. To live as a Eucharistic missionary is to begin to look for where God is on the move, where he has invited you into this drama, and to follow him in that work.

In the next chapter, we'll talk about how we do that.

Questions to pray with and ponder

- How does it make you feel knowing that the age of Christendom is over, and that the Church is being called once again to apostolic mission?
- Why is the Eucharist so essential to us for carrying out this mission in the world?

CHAPTER 9
Making His Mission Our Own

At the end of Mass, we hear the words, "The Mass has ended, go in peace." The missional mandate of the Eucharist is always in front of us, articulated so clearly. The Mass itself derives its name from the sending forth that traditionally happened at its end: *Ite missa est* ("Go, she [the Church] has been sent"). But this missional mandate can be hard. What does it mean? Go where? To whom? How?

To answer these questions, we will take as our exemplar Mary, the first evangelist. She is the great image of evangelization, showing us the fullness of what it means to live mission, a perfect balance of the relationship between receptivity to God and action.

Consider the accounts we hear of Mary. She is constantly on the move, pressing into this work of laboring to bring about the Kingdom with her son. As soon as the angel tells her she will bear the Son of God, she rushes to Elizabeth, both to share the good news with her and to minister to her in her own pregnancy. Mary's gaze is outward, focused on the needs of others. At Cana she notices a need — the couple's embarrassing lack of wine for their guests — and she makes a decision, with her son, to step out of the joy and peace of Nazareth into the turbulence of the next phase of Jesus' ministry. "They have no wine," she tells Jesus (see Jn 2:3), and she continues to bring our needs to him today, as she helps guide the Church.

At the cross, Mary walks every step of the way with her son. Even in this moment of grief and loss, he entrusts her with a new mission: to take care of and build up John, the beloved friend of Jesus, who will lead a local church and uniquely communicate who the Son of God is to the world.

At Pentecost, we find Mary right in the heart of the action. As the apostles pray in the Upper Room for nine days, symbolic of nine months of pregnancy, the Church is born in their fasting and prayer. Mary, who once birthed the Savior of the world, now participates in this spiritual birth of the Church, inviting her spouse, the Holy Spirit, to inaugurate the Kingdom.

Mary is the Eucharistic missionary par excellence. It was her example that so inspired Mother Teresa, who said:

Every holy Communion fills us with Jesus, and we must, with Our Lady, go in haste to give him to others. For her, it was on her first holy Communion day that Jesus came into her life, and so for all of us also. He made himself the Bread of Life so that we, too, like Mary, become full of Jesus. We too, like her, should be in haste to give him to others. We too, like her, serve others.[1]

What does this look like in our own lives? In this chapter, we offer four steps to beginning to live out the mission of the Eucharist — to make the mission of Jesus in the Eucharist our own.

Step 1: Cultivate zeal for souls and a missionary heart

Mission, if it is to be authentic, should be a value response to the person in front of us. Catholics do not just love humanity; we love persons. Pope St. John Paul II put it this way: "A person's rightful due is to be treated as an object of love."[2] To recognize the person in front of us is to see someone who is worthy of love. We have not recognized the person in front of us until we see them as worthy of love from us, in a way that costs us something. Only then do we see people as they really are, which leads us to long for their good.

We actively cultivate this disposition toward other people by practicing the discipline of considering what C. S. Lewis called "the weight of my neighbor's glory."

In June 1941, as Europe was being thrown into World War II, Lewis delivered an important sermon. In the midst of a discouraging time, he chose to focus, in a sweeping and grand treatise, on the eternal destiny of humankind:

> It may be possible for each to think too much of his own potential glory hereafter; it is hardly possible for him to think too often or too deeply about that of his neighbor. The load, or weight, or burden of my neighbor's glory should be laid daily on my back, a load so heavy that only humility can carry it, and the backs of the proud will be broken. It is a serious thing to live in a society of possible gods and goddesses, to remember that the dullest and most uninteresting person you talk to may one day be a creature which, if you saw it now, you would be strongly tempted to worship, or else a horror and a corruption such as you now meet, if at all, only in a nightmare. All day long we are, in some degree, helping each other to one or other of these destinations. It is in the light of these overwhelming possibilities, it is with the awe and the circumspection proper to them, that we should conduct all our dealings with one another, all friendships, all loves, all play, all politics. There are no ordinary people. You have never talked to a mere mortal. … Next to the Blessed Sacra-

ment itself, your neighbor is the holiest object presented to your senses.[3]

Being a Eucharistic missionary requires we see the world this way. For Mother Teresa, this was not fully possible unless we come to know the love of Jesus in the Eucharist. She said, "We must pray to Jesus to give us that tenderness of the Eucharist. Unless we believe and see Jesus in the appearance of bread on the altar, we will not be able to see him in the distressing disguise of the poor."

Over time, looking at others in this way becomes a habit, a disposition of our soul. Having encountered Jesus in the Eucharist, we are moved to seek the good of our neighbor, going swiftly, like Mary. We come to love the things that Jesus loves, which means we have true zeal for souls, and we move urgently, with haste, to draw others to Jesus' love.

Step 2: Allow ourselves to be led by the Holy Spirit

The Holy Spirit is the principal agent of evangelization. He leads and guides the Church in her mission. Living out Eucharistic mission means doing God's works with him and through him. Whenever we participate in the work of evangelization, we step into this great love story that formed the universe, conquered sin and death, and now invites all to live life to the full, through the Eucharist. But the work of mission is always ultimately God's work. Like the kid working on the car with his dad, we are being asked to participate in something that is beyond our comprehension and our own ability to accomplish.

We have no power to overcome the reign of sin and death in any human life. The mystery is that, in Jesus, we are invited to participate in his work of conquering sin and death. This profound mystery should fill us with two things: first, reverence for the gift, mystery, and freedom of the person in front of us; and second, peace, knowing that we can step into what God is asking us to do and be faithful to our efforts, trusting him with the outcome. This peace should be reinforced by the fact that we are able to actually receive him in the Eucharist and become more united to him and his work to rescue all.

In the Genesis account of creation, we read that in the beginning, the Spirit of the Lord hovered over the primordial waters of chaos and began to bring order to them. Today, even in the midst of so much hurt in our culture and in individual hearts, the Holy Spirit is constantly at work to bring order out of chaos. To follow the work of the Holy Spirit as a Eucharistic missionary, then, requires several things of us, especially:

- **Discernment in the Holy Spirit:** This means listening, learning in prayer and in life how to recognize his movements. If we do this, we will start to see "greater ones than these" (Jn 14:12). God will show up in our efforts to the extent that we trust that he will, and make space for him to do so.

- **Identification of our own charisms:** Part of what God is calling us to do in mission has been identified, already, in the ways he has uniquely created us. As baptized Catholics, we will recognize that we're able to do certain things with an ease that is beyond us, and these actions can have a big impact. These special gifts are called *charisms*, which we receive at our baptism so that we can uniquely participate in the redemptive work of God. The St. Catherine of Siena Institute (siena.org), and specifically its "Called and Gifted" training, is broadly recognized as one of the leading organizations in helping Catholics to identify and live out their charisms.

- **Docility and surrender:** As C. S. Lewis said, "To love at all is to be vulnerable."[4] Following the Holy Spirit is going to be uncomfortable sometimes, and it requires surrender. God will ask us to do things, give up things, and go places we did not expect. Our responsiveness and docility, even in small things, leads over time to God entrusting us with greater things.

We hand over our preferences, wishes, and comfort to the uncomfortable working of the Holy Spirit. This takes surrender and stepping out into the deep. Only in this way can we participate in all God has for us and for the world.

Step 3: Evangelizing by word

You have probably encountered this quote, often attributed (incorrectly) to St. Francis of Assisi: "Preach the Gospel at all times; if necessary, use words." If we are honest, one of the hardest parts of mission is using words to reach those who do not believe. Yet we must witness through our words, articulating the presence and goodness of Jesus in the Eucharist, so that others can experience his presence and goodness as well.

Witnessing through our words can be scary, because it could mean risking our relationship with the person to whom we speak. But think about it this way: If you had the cure for cancer, would you stay quiet about it, for risk of offending? We cannot let our fear of rejection keep us from speaking about God to others when the time is right. Too many today have misconceptions about the Faith and about Christians, whether from words left unsaid or words and actions that became a counterwitness to the radiant light of the Gospel.

The gift of Jesus in the Eucharist is great enough that it is worth sharing. If this really is the love of God poured out for every human person, the answer to every question and longing of the human heart, then how can we not share that?

We can witness through our words in many ways.

Here are just a few ideas:

- **Share your own experience of being rescued by Jesus.** Apologetic proofs for the Faith can be useful, but they're also easy to argue against. People can't argue with your own personal story. Most of us can't articulate the truths of the Faith the way a trained theologian can, but we can talk about how we have experienced God's pursuit of our souls. Spend time thinking about this and develop a way you can share your story simply and powerfully, when the time is right. Then, look for times when the Holy Spirit might be prompting you to share.

- **Make a monthly habit of asking God, "Who are the three people you are asking me to go to on mission right now in my life?"** Listen for his answer, and write down the three names he gives you. Pray for the three people each day throughout the month. Ask God to show you what these three people need most. Then, pray for wisdom to know how you can meet that need. Build or deepen your relationship with that person, sharing your faith openly, in a way they will be open to receiving. This is a simple habit that even busy Catholics develop to make sure that mission to others is always an intentional part of our lives. It's much more likely to happen if we schedule it and write it down.

- **Gather a small group to begin meeting regularly.** Everyone today needs more community. Creating a space for relationship with others and encounter with God can be a powerful way to live out our mission and be strengthened for evangelization. Often, in small groups, we are looking to be fed ourselves, seeking relationships with other dedicated Catholics. This is a great need — to put on our "oxygen mask" first and have a supportive community in this difficult time to be Catholic. However, in being open to evangelizing in word, we should also consider how God is inviting us to step out in leadership by gathering a small group that is not primarily about our experience of community, but how we can pour into others.

When I (Tim Glemkowski) was a new teacher in a Catholic high school, an older mentor figure invited me and two other young teachers into a discipleship group. He knew he was retiring soon and wanted to invest in some of the younger leaders in the school so we could continue the legacy of dynamic Catholic culture in the school. I will never forget the investment this teacher made in me. We might feel unworthy to step out in this way. It may make us feel uncomfortable and stretched, but God will bless our courage.

Step 4: Evangelizing by deed

When we consider mission, we tend to gravitate naturally toward either the corporal or the spiritual works of mercy. Depending on our temperament and formation, we are likely to find one of the two sets is more comfortable for us. Maybe I have multiple novenas going for different intentions for people in my life but do not feel as much of an inclination to meet the material needs of the poor. Or I love to minister to the homeless every week, but I struggle to share my faith verbally with others. Whatever our comfort zone looks like, the love of Christ calls us to perform both corporal and spiritual works of mercy.

Quoting St. Charles Borromeo, the *Catechism* reminds us,

> *The Eucharist commits us to the poor.* To receive in truth the Body and Blood of Christ given up for us, we must recognize Christ in the poorest, his brethren: You have tasted the Blood of the Lord, yet you do not recognize your brother. ... You dishonor this table when you do not judge worthy of sharing your food someone judged worthy to take part in this meal. ... God freed you from all your sins and invited you here, but you have not become more merciful. (1397)

Cardinal Francis George once famously said to a room full of wealthy people, "The poor need you to draw them out of poverty, and you need the poor to keep you out of hell."

This mission can look many different ways. It is worth re-listing here the corporal works of mercy to inspire our imagination with possibilities for living the Eucharistic mission of Jesus in the world today:

- Feed the hungry
- Give drink to the thirsty
- Visit those in prison
- Bury the dead
- Shelter the stranger
- Comfort the sick
- Clothe the naked

Jesus says: "Whoever has two tunics should share with the person who has none. And whoever has food should do likewise" (Lk 3:11). This is the heart of Jesus in the Eucharist for the poor, and, certainly, many of us have more than two shirts. Jesus in the Eucharist is asking us to join him on mission by serving our brothers and sisters, both spiritually and physically. We love people because we are Catholic, not because they are Catholic.

The mission of the Church is always somewhat different — not in degree but in kind — from the social work of the world. This is precisely because of the Eucharist. Our love for people in the world, which must at some point become action, is sourced and summited, like all else in our Church, in Jesus in the Eucharist. It is Catholic hearts, burning with charity, with love of God, that must overflow into love of neighbor. And likewise, all our efforts at mission ultimately must hold space, while ensuring we never proselytize, for the eventual invitation for those whom we serve to come to know the same love we have found: the love of Jesus in the Eucharist.

Out of its spiritual fullness and richness, then, even in spite of the perpetual human failings and weaknesses of those to whom it is offered, the Eucharist also sends us to meet the deep spiritual poverty of our time. Skyrocketing rates of mental illness show that we live in a moment where the spiritual works of mercy are uniquely needed. As we attend to the practical needs of the least, so must we be mercifully attentive to some of the deep spiritual hurts and needs of our time. We meet these needs by practicing the spiritual works of mercy:

- Counsel the doubtful
- Instruct the ignorant
- Admonish the sinner
- Comfort the sorrowful
- Forgive injuries
- Bear wrongs patiently
- Pray for the living and the dead

Living these spiritual works of mercy well is hard to do. If you have ever been severely wronged, and needed to bear that patiently, or to forgive after the fact, you know that these are no simple tasks for anyone.

To carry out these works, we need to be united with Jesus in the Eucharist. Maybe we are tempted to shy away from these spiritual hurts of the world, given how uniquely taxing it can be in our own life to walk with people whose hearts are hurting. To continue to walk with someone as they taste what Pope Benedict XVI called the "salt water of doubt,"[5] for example, and struggle with the truths of the Faith, can feel like hitting your head against a wall. Over years, as this struggle perhaps continues, it can be tempting to give up and to simply "not go there" anymore.

Jesus, in the Eucharist, enables our own hearts to continue to receive life as we engage with the world. In the Mass, Jesus takes the things of the world into himself and makes them into himself. He does the same for the pain found in the world today and enables us to carry it without losing our own peace. We can continue to walk with the grieving long after others think they should have moved on. We can lovingly and calmly call our brother or sister out of their sin, risking the relationship and overcoming our fear of their anger.

With Jesus in the Eucharist, we are sent to extend the peace he brings. This is not flowery pietism. The power of the resurrected Lord of the universe is such that, as he gives himself to me, I myself am able to go,

in prayer, in word, in action, to the manifold spiritual hurts in the world, armed with the conviction that
there may be something I can actually do about it. I am
sent, as he was sent, to

> bring good news to the afflicted,
>   to bind up the brokenhearted,
> To proclaim liberty to the captives,
>   release to the prisoners,
> To announce a year of favor from the LORD
>   and a day of vindication by our God;
> To comfort all who mourn. (Isaiah 61:1–2)

Our time calls for this kind of Eucharistic mission in a
particular way. And yet, instead, some of the toxic elements of subcultures on the Internet, especially certain social media influencers and divisive news outlets,
have convinced us that many who are experiencing
these hurts of the soul in the world are "bad." To live
out Eucharistic Mission means to see the world through
the eyes of Jesus in the Eucharist, as he gazes out on
the woundedness of the world, and to step into those
places with boldness and especially charity. We should
take care as we engage in the spiritual works of mercy
to always let love lead us. This love should lead us to
never shy away from the patient persistence often required to walk with someone whose soul is hurting in
various ways, and it should encourage us to adopt the
tenderness and attentiveness that a human person, and

the magnitude of their dignity, deserves.

Questions to pray with and ponder

- Which of the works of mercy (corporal and spiritual) come naturally to you? Which are more challenging? What is one more challenging work you can commit to practicing, starting now?
- To whom is Jesus inviting you to go on mission? How does that make you feel? What is one concrete way you can begin to answer that call?

CHAPTER 10

Becoming a Eucharistic Missionary

Each of us has an opportunity to be a part of the solution to the cry of the world right now. This requires, however, that we make a decision to live differently. Cardinal Joseph Ratzinger communicated this task powerfully in an address he gave to catechists during a gathering in the Jubilee Year 2000. He said:

> To evangelize means: to show this path — to teach the art of living. At the beginning of his public life Jesus says: I have come to evangelize the poor (Luke 4:18); this means: I have the response to your fundamental question; I will show you the path of life, the path toward happiness — rather: I am that path.
>
> The deepest poverty is the inability of joy,

the tediousness of a life considered absurd and contradictory. This poverty is widespread today, in very different forms in the materially rich as well as the poor countries. The inability of joy presupposes and produces the inability to love, produces jealousy, avarice — all defects that devastate the life of individuals and of the world.

This is why we are in need of a new evangelization — if the art of living remains an unknown, nothing else works. But this art is not the object of a science — this art can only be communicated by [one] who has life — he who is the Gospel personified.[1]

This is what it means to be a Eucharistic missionary: to receive life from Jesus — "the Gospel personified" — learning from him the "art of living," and then sharing him with others.

Is God calling me?

Two long-standing undercurrents may make us hesitant to answer Jesus' invitation to join him in his Eucharistic mission. The first is a sense of unworthiness. We know that we have done nothing to deserve the depth of God's love for us and his total self-gift to us in the Eucharist. In fact, the prayer we offer right before receiving holy Communion states that unequivocally: "Lord, I am not worthy that you should enter under my roof, but only say the word and my soul shall be healed."

But this should not discourage us. After all, none of us is worthy of what God longs to give us. The good news is that God counts us worthy anyway. Even more, the transforming power of the Holy Spirit is within us, working to make us worthy. It's good to be God's humble servants. The self-doubt that we face is simply a lie from the enemy, telling us we aren't holy enough to bring Jesus to others. We can cast aside that lie and lean into the truth of who we are in Christ.

The second undercurrent is the notion that everyday Catholics are unqualified to act as missionary disciples. We may believe that mission is best left to the "professionals." Consider, however, that those closest to Jesus weren't highly educated, particularly strong, very rich, or extraordinarily skilled. He called them anyway, and then sent them out to continue his mission, first two by two (see Mk 6:7–13), and then, "to the ends of the earth" (Acts 1:8). In baptism, each one of us was called by name, just as the first disciples were. Every Christian is called by Jesus. And while we will serve God in different capacities and according to the gifts he has given us, we all have the ability to serve him. All of us are missionary disciples. All of us are sent.

But how do we make this practical? We need to know how to commit to this new life day in and day out, week in and week out. While much will depend on individual circumstances and discernment, we can offer some specific suggestions for living as a Eucharistic missionary. These suggestions fall into three categories: Holiness, Community, and Mission.

1) Commitment to personal holiness

Mother Teresa had a powerful commitment to spending time with Jesus in the Eucharist, and, in slowly surrendering her heart to him, her life was changed. In fact, knowing the great mission work she accomplished, you would be shocked to see how much of her day she spent in rhythms of prayer, community life, and rest. The work of her mission to the least and the lost that would make her famous across the world took up about seven hours each day. How easy it would be to slip into workaholism! But Mother Teresa knew that everything depended on God anyway, so time spent in prayer was not wasted.

For Mother Teresa, Venerable Fulton Sheen, and other saints, a daily Holy Hour and daily Mass were the cornerstones of this life of prayer. For us, that might not be realistic. This does not stop God from still being able to work deeply in our hearts. However, if we feel the Lord tugging on our hearts, inviting us to live as Eucharistic missionaries, we must adopt fruitful rhythms of life as well, rooted in prayer. In particular, we should commit to:

- **Daily prayer:** Set time aside every day — at least fifteen minutes, just one percent of your day — just for Jesus, to open your heart to his presence and encounter him in his word.

- **Daily Mass:** As often as possible, attend the sacrifice where you can receive the Eucharist, and where your heart is conformed to Jesus' self-gift. Consider whether you can attend Mass at least one day during the week, in addition to your Sunday commitment.

- **Weekly adoration:** Every week, if you can, spend time before Jesus' living presence in Eucharistic adoration and allow him to shape you. Over time, if your parish has an adoration chapel, commit to a regular, weekly Holy Hour, if your life allows for such a commitment.

- **Monthly confession:** Regularly seek his mercy so you can become more and more like him.

2) Commitment to a life of communion

As we talked about in chapter 6, to live in communion with Jesus and to carry out the mission he gives us, we need friends. There is a special closeness of friendship that comes when we run the race of holiness with others. Eucharistic missionaries need friends with whom they can be vulnerable, find accountability, and receive encouragement to keep going. This can happen through small groups or other intentional communities, many of which are already growing throughout parishes and dioceses. This intentional sharing of Christian life is essential to sustain us in our Eucharistic mission, and as we commit to it, it becomes one of the greatest sources of joy.

This life of communion is not just with the Church here on earth, but also with those in heaven. A Eucharistic missionary must also cultivate devotion to the Blessed Mother and the saints. As we read the lives of the saints, we find great help in imitating their deep love for the Eucharist and their courage in witnessing that love. Meditating on the life of Mary and the saints will teach us more and more how to surrender our lives to Jesus.

Living the communion of a Eucharistic missionary, then, would entail:

- **Sharing life with other Catholics:** In or out of the parish, in a small group setting, wherever it happens, someone committed to a deeper conformity to Jesus in the Eucharist would commit to stable and regular relationships of friendship that would allow for both accountability and vulnerability.
- **Devotion to Mary:** Mary always leads us to her Son, fully present in the Eucharist. Growing in our relationship with Mary through devotions such as the Rosary, the Total Consecration to Mary according to St. Louis de Montfort, or praying the Memorare, are powerful ways to live out the re-

lationship she offers to us!

- **Devotion to the Saints:** The saints are our friends, cheering us on and interceding for us. A Eucharistic missionary will find a way to cultivate special devotion to some saints, to invite them to run the race with us, and to learn about their lives to understand what a life conformed to Jesus in the Eucharist looks like.

3) Commitment to a life of mission

To be a Eucharistic missionary means to seek to accompany the lost, last, and least. This requires a personal commitment to witness in word and in deed. If we want to grow in our Eucharistic mission, we should commit, even if it is in a small way, to at least one work in evangelization and one in service. Here are some practical suggestions for making this commitment.

- Keep a list of just two or three people to whom God is currently sending you in a unique way. Pray for those people. Ask God what he wants you to do in their lives.
- As an examination of conscience, pray a couple of times each year intentionally, perhaps with special consideration prior to Lent as one of those times, with the corporal and spiritual works of mercy. Ask God where he is calling you to devote your life

to address the hurt of the world in a deeper way.

- Undertake some process to pray specifically with your particular charisms. What has God specifically blessed you to do for him? Consider how those charisms might be used to build up the Church and the world. Be not afraid.

In this way, through a life of holiness, communion and mission, all flowing from and returning to Jesus in the Eucharist, we can become true Eucharistic missionaries, conforming our lives to the merciful, Eucharistic heart of Jesus, and joining him in rushing to respond to the pain of the world.

Questions to pray with and ponder

- What makes you hesitate to see yourself as a missionary? Is it fear, or a sense of your own weakness, or something else? Do you believe that Jesus in the Eucharist wants to help you step into this role?
- Do you already have a devotion to a particular saint (or saints)? If yes, who is it, and what is it about that saint's life that attracts you? If no, ask the Holy Spirit to guide you to the saint (or saints) he has in mind to help you carry out your unique mission.

Conclusion

The history of the Church proves that when times are darkest and seem most difficult, God works most powerfully and supernaturally. From the time of the apostles, we can perceive this truth. Waves of persecution in the first centuries of Christian faith did not stifle the spread of the Gospel. Heresies did not compromise the truth revealed in Christ and his Church. Amidst the rise and fall of civilizations, discord and corruption (even within the Church), revolutions and reformations, disasters and wars: God's plan of redemption has continued to unfold, and his presence in his Church lives on. God has always kept his promise to remain with us, and even to make all things new. When things are most dire, God works most dramatically.

One of the greatest examples of this happened in the sixteenth century with the apparition of Our Lady of Guadalupe. The Aztec culture in Mexico was one of the most antilife cultures that ever existed. Their religious worship consisted of daily human sacrifice. In many ways, it was the epitome of what Pope St. John Paul II called a "culture of death."

When Spanish conquistadors came to Mexico early in the sixteenth century, they were horrified. They shut down the practice of human sacrifice, but they could not convert the Aztecs to faith in Christ. Why? Because they themselves were also evil, in how they treated the indigenous peoples. Their lives were at odds with the Gospel they claimed to believe. Franciscan missionaries attempted to bring Christianity to the Aztecs, but their efforts were thwarted by the cruelty of the Spanish soldiers. The first bishop of Mexico, Juan de Zumárraga, grew exasperated as he tried to get the Spanish soldiers to treat the natives with the dignity they deserved. He wrote a letter to the king of Spain at the beginning of December 1531, explaining how dire the situation was and asking him to control the soldiers. He wrote, "If God does not provide the remedy from his hand, the land is about to be completely lost."

Within days, God's hand provided a remedy. On December 9, 1531, Our Lady of Guadalupe appeared to Juan Diego on Tepeyac Hill, and the largest and quickest conversion of peoples in the history of the world followed. Nine million indigenous people became Catholic within ten years. When times are darkest, God acts most powerfully.

It is no accident that the bishops of the United States use the word *revival* as they speak about the renewal in Eucharistic faith that we need today. Although the word is more familiar to Pentecostals, there are revivals throughout biblical and Catholic history. Many times the prophets, from Hosea to Elijah, called people back to the covenant of God, and often God inspired the people to respond with repentance and revival. Think of the example of revival that occurred when Haggai and Zechariah called the Jewish people to rebuild the Temple. In fact, Pentecost itself was a revival that saw the conversion of thousands in one day.

Bill Bright, an evangelical pastor and founder of Campus Crusade for Christ, gave an excellent description of revival, which is useful in our Catholic context for understanding these uncommon times of God's action. He said:

> During a revival God will:
> 1. Grip his people with deep conviction, repentance, forgiveness, and deliverance from personal sins.
> 2. Fill his people with the Holy Spirit and manifest through them the fruit and graces of the Holy Spirit.
> 3. Fill the church and community with his presence and power.
> 4. Cause non-Christians to earnestly seek him.
> 5. Ignite in his people, young and old, a passion to bring the lost to Christ at home and around the world.[1]

We believe that this is what God desires to do in our world today, and that he wants to use us to do it. Only God can bring about a revival, which is the work of the Holy Spirit. But we can be like Bishop Zumárraga, begging for help from heaven.

We believe that the Eucharist is the answer to the problems of our world, because the Eucharist contains the entire spiritual wealth of the Church: Christ himself. And so we turn to Christ in the Eucharist, knowing that without him all will be lost. And with firm faith that he is the light in the darkness of this world, we beg him to make us his missionaries. We beg him to form us in the Eucharistic life that he himself lived, so that we might give ourselves, too, for the life of the world.

Notes

Chapter 1: Starting a Fire

1. See *Catechism of the Catholic Church* (Washington, DC: United States Catholic Conference, Inc.—Libreria Editrice Vaticana, 1994), par. 1. Subsequent references to the *Catechism* will be cited parenthetically in text as "CCC."

2. Pope Francis, General Audience, May 24, 2017.

Chapter 3: Who Is Jesus and What Did He Come to Do?

1. Pope Benedict XVI, *Deus Caritas Est*, vatican.va, par. 1.

Chapter 4: Encounter Changes Everything

1. Pope Francis, *Desiderio Desideravi*, vatican.va, par. 10.

2. Benedict XVI, *Deus Caritas Est*, par. 1.

3. Pope Francis, *The Name of God is Mercy* (New York: Random House, 2016), 34.

4. Mother Teresa, "Varanasi Letter," March 1993.

5. St. Augustine of Hippo, *Enarrationes in Psalmos* 98:9,

CCL XXXIX, 1385.

6. Second Vatican Council, *Lumen Gentium*, vatican.va, par. 11.

Chapter 5: Eucharistic Identity

1. Pope St. John Paul II, *Redemptor Hominis*, vatican.va, par. 10.

2. Second Vatican Council, *Gaudium et Spes*, vatican.va, par. 22.

3. John Paul II, *Redemptor Hominis*, par. 10.

4. Pope St. John Paul II, *Nuovo Millennio Inuente*, vatican.va, par. 15.

5. John Paul II, *Nuovo Millennio Inuente*, par. 34.

6. Second Vatican Council, *Sacrosanctum Concilium*, vatican.va, par. 10.

7. Second Vatican Council, *Presbyterorum Ordinis*, vatican .va, par. 5.

Chapter 6: Eucharistic Life,
Part 1: Living in Communion

1. Vatican II, *Lumen Gentium*, par. 11.

2. Benedict XVI, *Deus Caritas Est*, par. 13.

Chapter 7: Eucharistic Life,
Part 2: Living Sacrificially

1. Louis Bouyer, *The Liturgy Revived: A Doctrinal Commentary of the Conciliar Constitution on the Liturgy* (South Bend, IN: University of Notre Dame Press, 1964), 23.

2. Sofia Cavalletti, *Living Liturgy: Elementary Reflections*,

trans. Patricia A. Coulter and Julie Coulter (Catechesis of the Good Shepherd Books, 1998), 12.

3. Francis, *Desiderio Desideravi*, vatican.va, par. 7.

4. Pope Benedict XVI, *Sacramentum Caritatis*, vatican.va, par. 71.

5. Elisabeth Leseur, *The Secret Diary of Élisabeth Leseur: The Woman Whose Goodness Changed Her Husband from Atheist to Priest* (NH: Sophia Institute Press, 2002).

6. Benedict XVI, *Sacramentum Caritatis*, par. 52.

7. Vatican II, *Lumen Gentium*, par. 11.

8. Vatican II, *Presbyterorum Ordinis*, par. 5.

9. Wilfrid Stinissen, OCD, *Bread That Is Broken*, trans. Sr. Clare Marie, OCD (San Francisco: Ignatius, 2020), 60.

Chapter 8: Eucharistic Mission

1. Second Vatican Council, *Dei Verbum*, vatican.va, par. 2.

2. Pope St. John Paul II, *Redemptoris Missio*, vatican.va, par. 34.

3. Francis, *Desiderio Desideravi*, par. 5.

Chapter 9: Making His Mission Our Own

1. Talk to the Brothers and Co-workers, Los Angeles, U.S.A., 1 July, 1977, quoted in Fr. Sebastian Vazhakala, MC, "The Holy Eucharist in the life of Bl. Teresa of Calcutta," EWTN, https://www.ewtn.com/catholicism/library/holy-eucharist-in-the-life-of-bl-teresa-of-calcutta-5528.

2. Karol Wojtyla, *Love and Responsibility* (San Franciso: Ignatius, 1993).

3. C. S. Lewis, *The Weight of Glory* (NY: HarperOne, 2001,

originally published by Geoffrey Bles, 1949).

4. C. S. Lewis, *The Four Loves* (NY: HarperOne, 2017, originally published by Geoffrey Bles, 1960).

5. Pope Benedict XVI, *Introduction to Christianity* (San Francisco: Ignatius, 1990), 20.

Chapter 10: Becoming a Eucharistic Missionary

1. Joseph Ratzinger, "The New Evangelization," Address to Catechists and Religion Teachers, December 12, 2000.

Conclusion

1. Bill Bright, quoted in Mary Healy, "What Does Eucharistic Revival Look Like?" *National Catholic Register*, February 22, 2023, https://www.ncregister.com/commentaries/what-does-eucharistic-revival-look-like.

About the Authors

Bishop Andrew Cozzens taught sacramental theology as a seminary professor and formator when he was named auxiliary bishop of St. Paul and Minneapolis by Pope Francis in 2013, where he served until being named bishop of Crookston, in Minnesota, in 2021. As chair of the Committee on Evangelization and Catechesis for the United States Conference of Catholic Bishops, he has led the bishops' three-year National Eucharistic Revival and is the chair of the board for the 10th National Eucharistic Congress.

Tim Glemkowski is CEO of the National Eucharistic Congress, Inc. An author, speaker, and consultant, Tim has worked in parish, apostolate, and diocesan roles related to the renewal of the Church for a time of apostolic mission. He lives in Littleton, Colorado, with his wife, Maggie, and their four young children.

You might also like:

My Daily Visitor: Eucharist
By Fr. Patrick Mary Briscoe, OP

Grow closer to Christ in the Eucharist with *My Daily Visitor: Eucharist*. This handy devotional with forty reflection themes helps you to pray and reflect on the source and summit of our Catholic Faith.

For each entry, Fr. Patrick Briscoe, OP, offers a brief reflection on a particular quote from a saint and concludes with a prayer. Reflection themes include the Real Presence, breaking of the bread, the Lamb's Supper, and more. This devotional also contains a collection of prayers before the Eucharist written by saints.

Perfect for Eucharistic adoration, prayer groups, and personal quiet time, *My Daily Visitor: Eucharist* will help enliven your relationship with Jesus in the Eucharist.

Available at
OSVCatholicBookstore.com
or wherever books are sold